GW00670504

index

This is not a book about one thing, this is a book about many things.
These things all amount to the most important thing:

It is not only about good food and setting the table beautifully,
it's about the way you feel when you do it.
Love is what makes the magic.
Love is what tastes so good.
Love is what glows.
The thoughts in this book, the words on these pages,
I could not have written them without Love.
Love is my pen.
This book is about Love in life,
Love in living, Love in Loving.

LOVE

How To Feed A Man

This Book is for My Beloved Man

L

Darling You,
You're All the Man I've ever Wanted…
… And yet somehow, You've made that More.
Thank You.

Always Your Butterfly,

S x

Foreword

Marco Pierre White

First impressions always count.
Firstly, the sexiest cookery book I have ever cast my eyes over…

Secondly, I liked the way it was put together.
Not too serious and therefore dissolves the fears and
makes you want to cook.

The eye was constantly amused.
A book in my opinion, constructed by a proper woman
who knows how to capture her man's imagination.

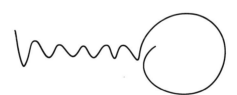

THE IMPORTANCE OF KITCHEN ESSENTIALS

Here I give you a list of things I always have in my kitchen. These things I cannot be without, as for me they are all too important. Not only do they make life easier, but for the way I live, the way I cook, the way I serve, they are part and parcel of my everyday life, and I humbly thank each and every item.

Big Serving Plates

An absolutely MUST have. A great big serving plate or, better still, plates. This is something I use for most of my recipes. Not only does it look fantastic to serve food that way, but I also believe it encourages people to drop any self consciousness, and relax and 'share', as ultimately sharing is just what you are doing, and to share food is a lovely thing to do. To me, it's happy and warm.

Big plates don't need to be a terribly expensive number either. There are many places one can find them – markets, antique shops, as well as the big high street chains. It really doesn't matter either if your big plate doesn't match the rest of your serving plates so long as it has the same sort of 'feeling' about it. By this I mean you wouldn't put a big chunky terracotta plate with a delicate service; but with a rustic one, fantastic.

How nice too if you got your big plate from some little remote village you crossed on your travels… It then becomes a conversation piece too. So, Big Plate, Big Winner all round!

Ps. If you don't have one, and your man cannot understand your need to buy one, (or carry one across a country's border) simply wait till he's hungry, entice him with a sweet smile and a delicious, mouth-watering food image, and when he's almost at dribbling point say: "Yes Darling, I would love to make that for you" … big sigh … "such a shame I can't as I don't have the Big Plate I need to serve it on…"

Big Wide Bowls

Now I believe pasta should be served in a bowl. This is how the Italians do it, and I think they have good reason. If you think about it, you're supposed to eat pasta with a fork and spoon, and perhaps a lovely hunk of bread (in for a penny, in for the pounds). The side of the bowl makes life much easier to roll the spaghetti onto your fork, also helping to keep the sauce on it, the sauce being what makes the pasta special. Even with penne pasta it's easier because you can eat without missing anything tasty, and use the bowl as an aid to balancing that last tomato on top of that last piece of pasta… like I say, the Italians eat like this for a clever and good reason.

Griddle Pans

Fantastic thing the griddle pan, really groovy. As close to an inside BBQ as you can get. You can cook any kind of meat, or even fish... steaks, chicken, lamb chops, veal, big fat prawns – I can't tell you how often I use mine. It's also good because you can get it hot hot hot and smokin', yet because of the weight of it, it doesn't burn the food, but instead gives it a great colour (nothing worse than a grey lamb chop, yuck), and the more you use it the better it gets. It never really cleans up shiny and perfect, and this is a good thing. There is nothing clinical about the griddle pan... Thank Goodness!!

Mixing Bowls

Like everything on this list, these really are very important. I mean, what would you do without them? The mind boggles... Anyway, it's best if you can have a couple of big glass ones (Pyrex), and smaller ones too. If you can also get a metal one, or two, all the better. Egg whites like metal ones, though copper is their favourite. Of course you can whisk egg whites in a glass bowl, but if you can make an egg white happy, then why not? If you're gonna make a cake, a big bowl is needed. I got mine years ago from a little antique market, and me and my beautiful bowl have been friends ever since, but you can get big solid mixing bowls from good kitchenware shops, and at the same time, perhaps pick up a couple of cake tins. You'll get a happy feeling buying cake tins. Even if you don't rush home and bake, and even if you don't bake very often, on the day you do you'll be so pleased you have one. Honestly, the time you feel like baking is the time you need to reach for the tin, and if it's there... "If I knew you were comin' I'da baked a cake, ah, baked a cake... baked a cake"!

Fish Slice

Must have. If you can, try to get a large one with some flexibility in it, as well as a totally rigid one but I do recommend you have one regardless, how else are you going to pick up that lovely big fish? The only thing you must not do is buy a floppy plastic one. Absolutely no merit in this whatsoever. Silly thing in plastic.

Spatula

These come in different sizes, and now colours too, how sweet is that? But I think bigger is better, and also one that is made of a firm plastic. Firm is better than not in most areas of life, and I'd say the same applies here!

Salt

The ONLY salt I use is MALDON SEA SALT. Looks more like sea flakes left by crashing waves on big boulders at the sea front... I cannot stress enough the difference between this lovely stuff and the tiny grains you find in salt cellars. It's strange, but this marvellous Maldon does not seem to have the same overpowering and extreme saltiness as others.

I ALWAYS have a little bowl of these wonderful flakes next to where I cook, and for whatever I'm cooking. It's much easier to control the amount you use, because you just pinch and crumble...

I suppose the closest thing would be rock salt, which if you had to choose between tiny grains or rock salt, rock would win every time (takeaway Fish and Chips being the exception), but trust me, these flakes are in a class of their own.

After opening

LLLY 17

Dé

5416245

rture, conserver au réfrigérateur

Kikkoman Teriyaki

Great stuff this.

You can find Teriyaki in most big, and some small, supermarkets. It's something I have in my store cupboard always. It's so versatile. Wonderful in a marinade, but also fantastic in a sauce...

There are different kinds, though, one thicker and sweeter than the other. I generally buy the Kikkoman Japanese brand. When you buy it, TASTE it, straight from the bottle. It's important to know what ingredients you are using – for whatever purpose – taste like. I use this in many sauce/marinade recipes.

Mustards...

I think it's important to have at least 3 different kinds of mustards...

1) Good old-fashioned Colman's English Mustard

The ready-to-use jar form, AND the Mustard Powder. Colman's mustard is great for beef – the powder and flour on the roast before cooking, the mustard with a nice big steak. Better yet, coupled with Ketchup on a plate of juicy sausages... and perhaps a Bloody Mary to accompany them both... Does it get any better ?!

2) Wholegrain Dijon Mustard

Always try to buy the most authentic of these French Mustards that you can. I have been using the 'Grey Poupon' brand for years, and to me, it's the best. Again, widely available in most good supermarkets. This mustard is wonderful in dressings, and goes particularly well with Balsamic Vinegar.

3) Dijon Mustard

Again, the 'Grey Poupon' brand is the best to my mind, though another really good one is the 'Mille', which is lovely, but a little stronger. With meat, if you don't want anything with as much kick as English, the Dijon is the softer version. It's also a must-have for marinades, and I often use the Dijon and Teriyaki together – in salad dressings, beautiful, particularly with a lovely red or white wine vinegar. I suppose as the French intended.

The other mustard you can get is Frenchies American Mustard. This, although great on burgers and hot dogs, is mainly for the kids, which I think is a good thing because it encourages them not to be frightened to try something that they thought they would hate, but actually like. Kinda like 'breaking them in gently' to the whole mustard-eating experience.

Olive Oil

Now with olive oil I really do think you need to have more than one. I kind of look on olive oil as I would red wine. There are so many flavours, some more subtle than others, and some more suited to certain foods than others. For example, a beautiful Virgin Olive Oil, Italian, Spanish or Greek, may have many strong and distinctive tastes, and some drizzled over mozzarella and tomato, fantastic, but completely wrong to use in a Shepherd's Pie... I say this because I actually made a whole Shepherd's Pie once with a lovely peppery olive oil, not thinking once what tragedy would occur, and had to throw the whole lot away because the oil completely overpowered the taste! What a waste!

Now what I do, and strongly suggest you do too, is buy several wonderful Olive Oils – Virgins to not so virtuous – and TASTE each one, and use them accordingly. Believe me, you are not being frivolous by doing this, though it may seem extravagant. There is nothing better then having a small selection of lovely oils, and using the best one to suit your dish.

Olive Oils. Perhaps think of them as shoes... You can have many different outfits, but you need at least 3 pairs of shoes to make sure you can look fabulous wearing anything, from Bikini to Black Tie!

Also, what a great present a beautiful bottle of Olive Oil makes...x

Vinegars...

There are so many vinegars out there, but basically what you need is a good red vinegar, be it the red wine or raspberry variety and a white wine vinegar. Again, the more authentic, the better. If you happen across a little shop and see a particular brand you've never seen before, and it looks like it should come with an old man on a bike wearing a necklace of onions, buy it! Vinegar lasts quite a long time, so it's worth the expense if it's a good one. In fact, if you do find a really good one that you love, buy 2 bottles, nothing more frustrating than not being able to get something that you love and use and can't find anymore...

Balsamic...

Somebody once told me that with Balsamic you simply have to go for the most expensive if you want the best, and I think on the whole, this is true. C'est la vie. But, like olive oils, if you buy more than one, one more expensive than the other, you can use them for different things, saving the really beautiful one for certain dishes... Either way, TASTE them all to give you an insight as to how sweet or sharp they are. Doing this is so, so important.

Butter

What can I say?
I'm a salted butter freak.
Anchor all the way for me... even cakes!

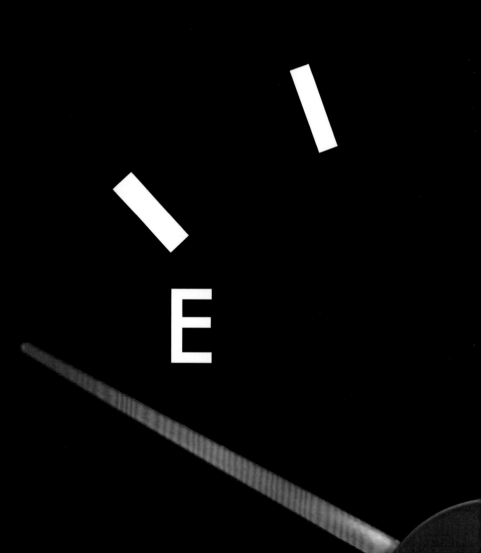

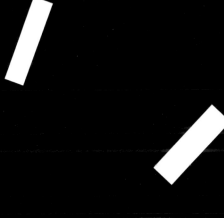

Teriyaki Chicken

I have been making this for many years now. I'm not entirely sure exactly where this recipe came from, I guess it's a kind of family mixture. Either way, it's terribly easy to make, and it never ever fails to get eaten; lunch, dinner, or cold the next day, it's an all-time winner! Great man and kid food!

Feeds 4 hungry boys, but like I say, any leftovers will soon disappear...

16 chicken thighs
¼ pint Kikkoman Teriyaki
Juice of 2 large or 3 small Lemons
2 heaped tablespoons Dijon Mustard
4 tablespoons Golden Syrup
2 level tablespoons Brown sugar
1 teaspoon crushed chillies
1½ fluid oz olive oil (optional)

Like I say I've been making this for so long now on auto pilot, so it was quite interesting to weigh it all out, but although I have given you exact measurements, nothing, I believe, unless you're baking a cake, is ever really exact, and after you've made this a few times, you won't even need me to tell you, you'll just know, that if you add a little bit more of this, or a little less of that, it doesn't matter, so long as it tastes great, and your family loves it, it will become YOUR chicken thing xx

Pre heat oven to hot, 230°C/450°F/Gas Mark 8, and pre heat the oven tray you'll be using at the same time. Put the chicken thighs in a large mixing bowl, and with a pair of scissors, just cut off any large pieces of excess fat on the thighs.

Next

Simply add all the remaining ingredients, get your hands in, and mix and massage away. You can, if you like, leave this sitting all day, or if needs be, cook it as soon as your oven is hot. Carefully put the chicken into the hot oven tray skin side up, and pour over any remaining marinade.

Cook it now for roughly 45 minutes, turning the temp down to 200°C/400°F/Gas Mark 6 after half an hour, during this time it's nice to turn the chicken several times to get the whole thigh coated in what becomes a lovely sticky sauce... Don't worry if toward the end the chicken starts to look quite dark, it's supposed to.

When your lovely tasty thighs are ready and you've got a room full of salivating creatures, make them wait. Just let it cool down and sit for a minimum of 10 minutes, loosely covered in foil. Honestly, people, doing this really makes a difference (plus the whole power trip on the hungry salivating creatures is fun).

Sometimes I make this for the kids, and if we are not eating with them, then I cover the chicken and leave it, and it's still lovely and warm by the time the bedtime story has been read. It's groovy making this for your little ones, and a casual dinner with friends, but to eat it after romance, sitting up on the kitchen counter, in the quiet, in the dark, fingers only... that's the best way.

Enjoy x

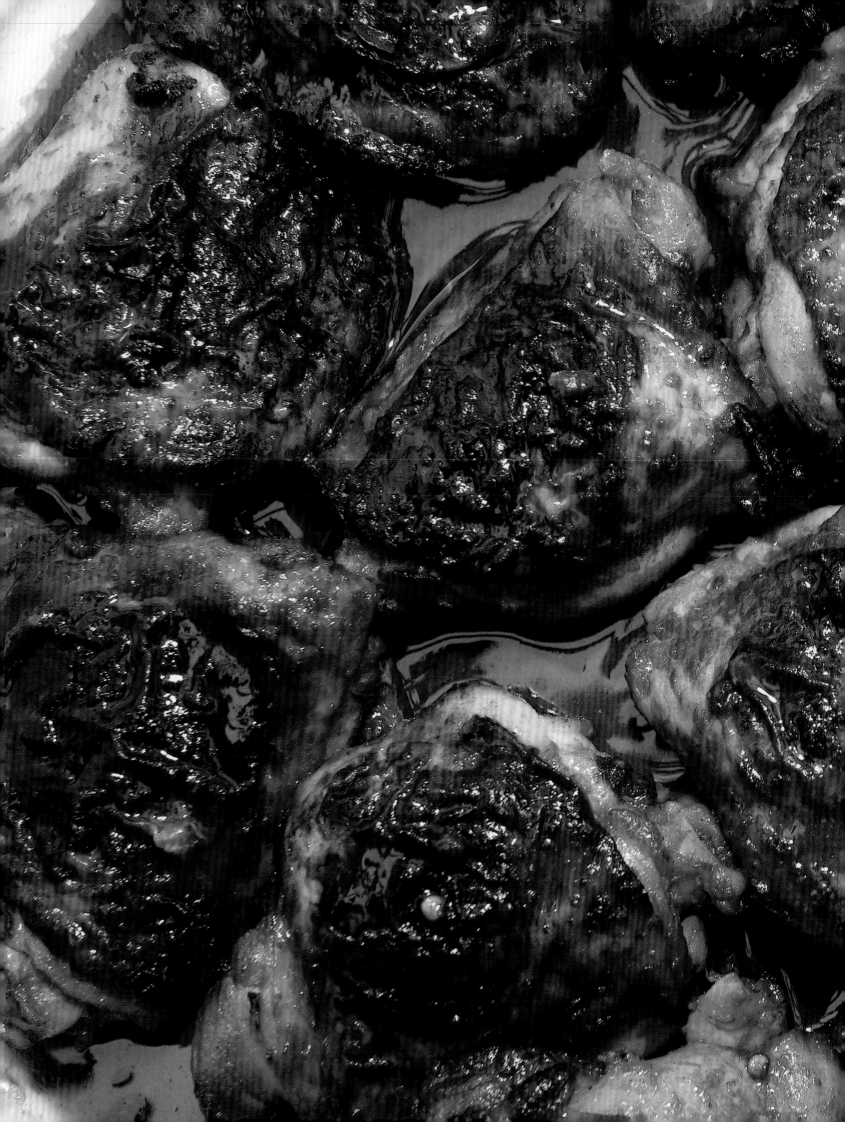

Made With Love

GROWING A CONFIDENCE

Growing a confidence is a
wonderful thing, and it is a thing that can
be grown.

It's a matter of bravery at first, then effort,
and then, without consciousness, an ease
appears, and your step is natural,
your confidence grown.
Really, it's so liberating,
it brings with it joy.

You really should try it.

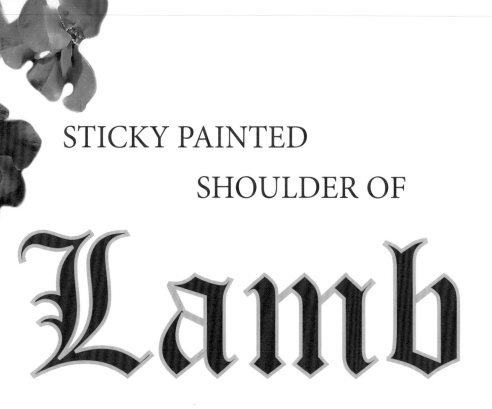

STICKY PAINTED SHOULDER OF Lamb

Ah this creation… I have to say, one of my best. Through trial and error came glory, and the glory was well received. Plus, you do actually 'paint' the lamb too, so even the mad artist in me was satisfied…

Slow cooked, sticky, incredibly tasty, hard to fail, the list of positives just goes on and on

Serves 4

Roughly 2 kilo Shoulder of lamb
Roughly 6 large potatoes
2 tablespoons Dijon Mustard
2 large lemons
Salt
Pepper
Olive oil to drizzle over

For the 'Paint'…

1 tablespoon crushed 'pimento'
cayenne chilli powder
1 tablespoon Sugar
1 tablespoon Tabasco
1 level tablespoon Maldon sea salt
1 heaped tablespoon tomato puree
Juice of 1 large lemon
2oz Olive oil
Little pasty brush

Pre heat your oven to 160ºC/310ºF/Gas Mark 3

Now before we start, bear in mind that this lamb, easy peasy and perfectly marvellous as it is, takes in all about 3 to 3½ hours to cook, and after cooking it can easily sit around quite happily for another half an hour to an hour, so it's something to make on a slow day, or else as soon as you get in the door from work. To be honest, the actual making of it is so hassle free, that so long as you have enough time for cooking and letting it sit for a bit, then make it whenever you want!

The first thing you do is put your lovely piece of lamb on a large oven tray and, with your hands, rub over the Dijon, lemon juice, olive oil and salt and pepper. That's it. First part finished. Now put it in the oven for 2½ hours, turning once after the first hour, and once again at the end.

During this time, you can make the paint. For some reason I always make mine in a large measuring jug, but a medium size mixing bowl will do just fine. Simply add all the 'paint' ingredients to the bowl, and mix together. You really must taste it 'cos it's magic! Keep your little magic paint brush next to it, ready and waiting…

Now just before your lamb has had its 2½ hours, take the potatoes, no need to peel, and slice them, in about a centimetre slice, lengthways, top to bottom. Take the lamb out of the oven, and place the potatoes around it in the oven tray, and even some under the lamb. Now it's painting time! Take the little brush, and simply paint the surface, sides, anywhere and everywhere you can, all over the lamb, and paint the potato slices too. Fantastic! You will probably find you have some paint left over, and this is good because you can repeat the painting process again in about 20 minutes…

Return the painted lamb and potatoes to the oven, and increase the oven temperature to 180°C/350°F/Gas Mark 4. Now, the remaining cooking time is about 40 to 50 minutes, during which time the paint will become sticky and caramelized, and the colour will deepen and change, from red to almost black (see I told you, magic paint). Halfway through this cooking time (20 minutes), take the lamb out, and paint again with any remaining sauce… **Mmmm, so lovely, it makes me hungry just thinking about it!**

Once the cooking time is up, take the lamb out of the oven, and cover the tray with tin foil till you're ready to eat, or leave it for at least 15 minutes….

So good, you really don't need anything else with it, but if you wanted, a simple green salad would suffice.
Enjoy ! x

NB: Obviously the cooking times will vary with different weights of lamb, but an extra hour/half an hour here and there is fine, just better to add that time at the beginning of the cooking as opposed to the end. x

pasta puttanesca

This has to be one of my favourite pastas. Not only does it have the most wonderful flavour, really rich and lovely, but it's quick and easy to make too. For some reason, probably because I have never had any problem finding ingredients wherever I am, this is always the first thing I make when we go away on holiday somewhere... so nice cold the next day too. x

Serves 6

1½ cloves garlic

Roughly 1 teaspoon dried chillies

2 x 500g passata tomatoes (basically pureed tomato sauce)

200g or 1 large tube tomato puree

1½ tins anchovies in olive oil

110g or 2 handfuls of pitted green or black olives

Olive oil

1 packet of Linguine pasta, or spaghetti pasta

Block of Parmesan cheese to grate

Crusty loaf

Butter

You'll notice that I haven't been too specific about the olives or chilli. This is because you can make it as **hot** or not as you **desire**, and add as many olives as you like, within reason!

Also, I make this sauce in a very large frying pan. I feel it's quite important to do this because it allows the sauce to cook quicker over a larger surface, and gets it all **thick** and **lovely**.

So, as always, get all the ingredients ready to hand. In particular, get the tomato Passata open and next to you. Put the frying pan over the heat, add olive oil and throw in the chilli. Then, using a garlic crusher, add the garlic (if you don't have a garlic crusher, chop the garlic as small as you can by hand). Then with a wooden spoon, stir that around for a few seconds, literally seconds, 'cos you don't want the garlic to burn. Now pour in the tomato Passata. It may splutter a little, so have your apron on!

Give that a good stir, add the purée, then turn the heat down. Next add the anchovies. There is no need to chop them, drain them or anything, just pull them out the tin, or jar using your fingers, and throw 'em in! Sometimes at this point I pour a **little** of the **oil** from the anchovy tin in too...

Stir gently, and as if by **magic**, the anchovies disappear! In fact, I am willing to bet that you wouldn't even know they are in there if you hadn't made it yourself (I can't tell you how many times I've made this for people who claim to hate these cute little fish, and the only comments I've had from them are along the lines of 'Please Sir, may I have some more...?'). **Of course** with a secret smile, **I willingly oblige!**

Stay with the heat turned to a right low. Leave it to cook, to a **gently bubbling simmer** for about half an hour, stirring occasionally.

Now with the olives, you need to roughly chop them, then rinse them under water. As perhaps you have noticed, we are not using any salt or pepper in this sauce. We already have the chillies for heat, and anchovies for salt, and as olives come in a brine, which is salty, we need to give them a good rinse. Please do taste the olives too, before and after you have rinsed them, and you'll get exactly what I mean. Don't be scared to give them a **gentle squeeze** and shake to get the water off them.

So after half an hour or so, throw the olives in, cook for a further **10 to 15 minutes** and your sauce is **ready**.

You can cover the sauce in the frying pan while you cook your pasta. Also, just throw the bread in the oven at this point, it will be **lovely and warm** by the time your pasta has cooked.

You can use either Spaghetti pasta, or Linguine Pasta (linguine being the kinda flatter skinnier version of spaghetti). Cook the pasta in a big pot of boiling water for the required time. Drain into a colander and put it back into the pot. This next bit is optional, and probably not **technically correct**, but I don't care about that, and I do it with all my pastas – add a **lovely big knob** of butter to the pasta, and **stir it around**. Then pour the sauce into the pot, and give the whole thing a **good mix**.

Delicious Italy at your table, served in big bowls with hunks of warm buttered bread… Strap it to your hips, baby!

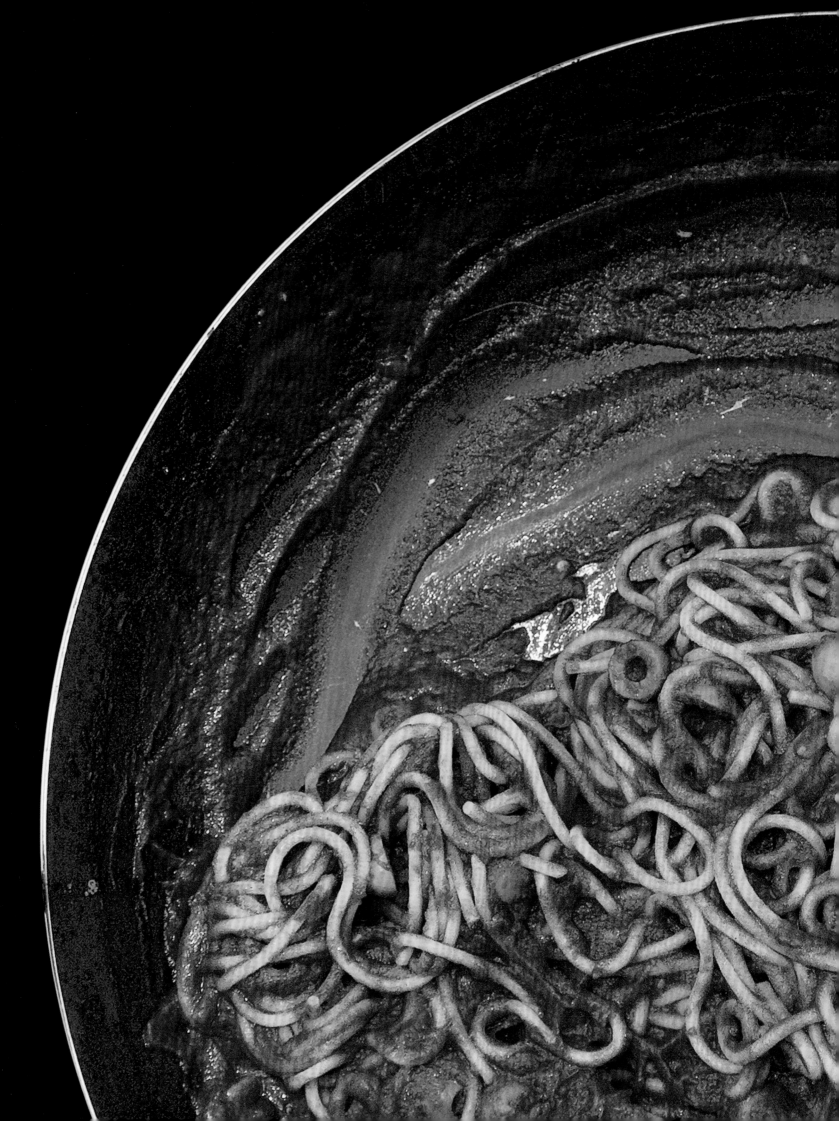

TIDY UP

Tidy up as you work. And I don't care how old fashioned or how boring it sounds, **DO IT**.

Want your stuff to turn out right?
Then tidy up as you go. It's the **ONLY** way to work.

You'll thank me, I promise. x

Robin's Cinnamon
POACHED PEARS

My lovely Robin is a very special man. Being the son of a farmer he's wonderfully English, and very proper. I remember him once making me a cup of tea and insisting he put the milk into a little jug, which I thought was absolutely marvellous. I just love people that care enough to make the effort, I wish there were more Robins about in this world of ours; people who know that little things make all the difference…

Anyway, I am lucky enough to have this beautiful old pear tree in my garden, and come summer, I end up with just about every kitchen surface covered in pears! Robin said to me, "Darling, for goodness sake, poach them!"… so I did, and my goodness it was easy and so delicious. In fact, my fella said it was his favourite ever dessert! Looks so beautiful too, it's great for a dinner party!

6 pears
1½ litres water
1 large cinnamon stick
2 cloves
2 tablespoons sugar

Fresh sprigs of
mint leaves
75gms dark chocolate
Double cream (just a little
to drizzle over)

First thing you do is peel the pears, leaving the little stork at the top. No need to core them. You may want to just cut a little off the underside of the pear so it sits nicely. Easy. Then place the pears in a medium-size saucepan, and pour over the water. Snap the cinnamon stick in half, and throw that and the cloves into the pan.

Next, bring the water up to boil, and then turn the heat right right down, so the pears are basically just sitting in very hot water. Think as if your pears have had a hard day, and you're just gonna leave them for the next 1½ to 2½ hours to soak in a lovely cinnamon-scented bath, all relaxed and happy; no need to cover them, stir them or anything. You can just occasionally turn them so that they get an even soak.

You can do this well in advance too, and your house will smell so wonderful. The first time I made these poached pears, I went upstairs to work, and actually thought someone had sprayed a lovely expensive room spray, or lit a scented candle! Really lovely…

...Now once the time is up,

(And you really don't have to be too precise about it, so long as they have had at least an hour and a half), gently take the pears out of the saucepan and put them to one side. Add the sugar to the poaching water, then turn the heat up and bring it to a boil. Boil for about 5 minutes or so, till the remaining water has reduced a little, and the taste intensified. Do taste it, it's absolutely wonderful! Strain the lovely scented syrupy water, into a bowl, then pour it back into your warm saucepan.

Place the pears back into the saucepan to keep cosy, and leave them there till you're ready to serve. You could actually just serve them as they are, in a little bowl with a couple of spoonfuls of the syrup, but if you are having a dinner party and want to be extra smart, here's what you do:

First, lay your dessert plates out ready, and get a little pan of boiling water on the go.

Next, re-heat the syrup and pears over a gentle heat, but don't worry if the pears are not very hot, they just need the littlest of warmth running through them. Take the mint leaves and choose each sprig so you have a lovely leaf on a little stalk, and push the stalk of the mint into the top of the pear where its natural leaf would have gone… So pretty.

Now, put your chocolate in a little bowl, place the bowl over the boiling water, and watch your chocolate melt! This takes literally a minute to do. Once melted, put a little circle of chocolate, about a spoonful, onto each plate, then carefully sit a pear on top of the melted chocolate, and gently press it down slightly so the chocolate helps it to stay standing up. Spoon a large tablespoon of the beautiful syrup gently onto the plate, and pour a little drizzle of cream onto the plate too.

Now children, walk very carefully to the table carrying your magnificent pear… as if you are carrying a piece of art… and you want it to stay just as you, my little Picasso, have created it!

It is my Privilege

I will try all my life to do the best for you;
It is my Privilege.
The loved around you will do their best for you, because it is your Love,
your Trust, that is given.

It will be an honour to Teach you, and for this fact I will endeavour to Listen
harder and Care more. Everyday.

I never dreamt for you because I never knew a Love this powerful could exist
outside myself.
But it does in you, and now I dream for you Everyday.

And I will see you, my Children,
Young in my Heart forever,
For sometimes it may be the way that you need me,
For I am your Mother, and it is my Privilege.

White Fish and Mash Potato

Originally, this recipe came from my children's Grandma. I would drop them off with her and they would run out of my arms and into hers, knowing that with her they would have love, security, and the kind of comfort that only Grandmas seem to have… If I were a poet, I would say that the softness and comfort of this dish, is like the softness and comfort of being held, cosseted, in Grandma's bosom, where fear has no place, where tears are dried, and where no matter how many years you have, the child in you still remains.

So today I still make this for my children, and they still love it, and because we all need a little comfort now and again, I make enough for me and my man too. xxx

Now, if you have any left over mash potato, this is the perfect time to make this.

Feeds 4

4 plump Cod Fillets, or Plaice Fillets	**Mash Potato**
½ Onion	**Desiree Red Potatoes**
Bay Leaf	**Loads of butter**
6 Peppercorns	**Splash of milk and/or cream**
¾ pint of Milk	**Salt**
Knob of Butter	
Pinch of Salt	

First make the mash.

NB: This is my basic mash potato recipe, and can be used when needed in other dinners. The only thing I'd say is that when you serve this as mash, no matter how much butter is in it, you absolutely MUST add a knob to the top once it's in its serving bowl. It simply isn't mash otherwise!

Big pot of boiling water on the stove. Peel and chop potatoes into chunks. Add them to the water, and throw in a hefty pinch of salt. Bring to boil, and boil for a good 20-25 minutes or until the potatoes are soft.

Drain the potatoes in a colander, and then leave them to dry out for a minute or two. It's important that you do this. I honestly believe this is the secret to great smooth mash. Next, put the potatoes back in the pot, making sure the pot is dry, and with your potato masher, mash like mad till you've broken up all the potatoes. Then add a massive chunk of butter, and mash some more. Then add another massive chunk of butter and mash like your hips are depending on you to burn enough calories to justify the food. Then, add a nice splash of milk, and what the hell, a splash of cream too!

Get a wooden spoon, and beat that creamy goodness in till your cheeks are pink. Taste, season, taste again. Add more of the above should you taste the need to. Now cover saucepan with a tea towel first, and a lid atop, till you're ready to use.

Now, Grandma's Fish...

Place the fish fillets in a medium saucepan. Next pour over the milk, should be enough to just about cover the fish, so if you feel you need to add a little more then by all means do so. Next, add the peppercorns, pinch of salt, bay leaf, the onion half and a nice knob of butter, and bring to simmering point, then turn the heat right down, so that only the occasional bubble rises to the surface. Now all you do is think nice things, and give the fish about 6 to 7 minutes to cook, depending on how fat your fillets are. During this time you can gently turn the fish over, but this is not absolutely necessary.

While you think nice things (start to warm up the mash potato if it's a leftover batch), get a lovely deep lipped serving plate ready. After the 6-7 minutes are up, if you gently prod the fish with a knife, you'll see that it will begin to flake beautifully, and you'll know it's ready, so take it off the heat. Spread your lovely creamy mash onto the serving plate, and then very gently, using a fish slice, put the fish fillets on top of the mash, being careful that you don't collect any peppercorns on the way. Please do not worry if the fish breaks up a little while you're transferring it; love and comfort have no sharp edges.

What I like to do as well, and what Grandma does, is spoon over some of that lovely warm milk that you have cooked your fish in.

Serve just as it is, or perhaps with some peas, but either way, and always, serve with love.

Sensitive Mushroom Risotto

I've called this sensitive, perhaps the better word would be 'delicate'.
It has the most lovely subtle flavours, yet it's rich and creamy and dreamy
and perfectly lovely... the only real fight it has is the Pecorino Cheese,
and even then, it's just a little unexpected but welcome jab.

Serves 2 hungry or 4 as a starter...

150gms Shimeji (Brown Beech) Mushrooms
50gms Oyster mushrooms
50gms Shiitake mushrooms
40ml Double Cream
1 medium onion (on the small side) very finely chopped
½ clove Garlic
Olive oil
Butter
Tablespoon finely chopped Flat Leaf Parsley
Up to 2 pints of water
2 Chicken Stock Cubes
8oz Arborio Rice
Small block of Pecorino Cheese
Medium size mixing bowl
Large Frying Pan
Large Heavy Saucepan
Ladle
Potato peeler, or cheese slicer

Now, before we start know this: Risotto is not something that can be rushed
at any stage of the game, the exception being when it's ready to be served.
So, if you're going to make this, be prepared to spend time nurturing and
loving what you're making, because although it's all about standing above
a pot and stirring, it's a very calming, pleasant way to spend 20-25 minutes.
And lovely too as each minute takes you a creamier step nearer the beautiful end.

OK, so have everything you need ready, parsley chopped and hot stock ready and cream weighed out before you start, and you start by gently frying the onions and garlic in olive oil until they are soft and golden. With the help of a spatula, put the cooked onions and garlic in to a bowl, and set aside.

Next, take the Shiitake and Oyster mushrooms, remove the stalk, and slice quite thinly, remembering that they shrink somewhat, but you don't want anything so big that it looks, well, 'insensitive'. Now with the Brown Beech Mushrooms, simple cut them away from the base they are attached to, but keep their long skinny stalks.

Put the frying pan back on the heat, and when it's hot, add a good splash of olive oil, and a lovely big knob of butter, and when the butter is foaming, add the mushrooms... Let those gorgeous guys soak up all that foam, and toss them around in the pan... After about 5 minutes or so, when the mushrooms are lovely and soft, throw in the parsley and give that a stir, then add the onion and garlic sitting in your little bowl to the mushrooms, season with salt and pepper, and stir in the double cream... Oh my Goodness me... this is Gorgeous... Cook for about 30 seconds or so, then pour the whole lot from the frying pan back into your bowl.

Now for the Risotto...

Place a big heavy base saucepan on the heat, add olive oil, a lovely bit of butter, and when that's almost melted, in goes your rice.

Take a lovely big wooden spoon and a smile, and as you stir just watch the rice embrace and draw all that olive oil and butter into its very soul... When the love affair is in full bloom, and the rice/butter/oil are as one, start to add the stock, slowly slowly, one ladle at a time of your chicken stock, stirring, stirring, waiting and watching the rice drink, and then again adding more, slowly, gently, all the while stirring, never letting the risotto go thirsty, but making it wait for the next drink (turn the heat down under your pan to a medium heat so it's simmering not boiling).

This process will take about 20 to 25 minutes, but when you get toward the 20-minute mark, taste the rice to see exactly what stage it's at. It should be almost there by now, and by this I mean soft, yet still with a little texture, but only needing a few minutes more cooking time. This is the point when you add that beautiful mushroom mixture to the pot, and let what was a love affair turn into a lifelong commitment of undying Love. Stir for perhaps a minute or so longer, and without burning yourself, taste for seasoning.

As soon as it's ready, spoon your Risotto into serving bowls, and using a potato peeler, shave some Pecorino Cheese over the top, and to the table you go...

Perfectly Lovely x

TUNA PASTA

This gorgeous pasta sauce came to me through a lovely lady that used to help me look after my little ones… So tasty was it that no matter how much they grow, they love it still. Really lovely cold the next day too, so whether you're packing a lunch box for your kids or your man, tuna pasta is a winner all round!

Serves roughly 4
500gs/1 carton of passata sieved tomatoes
4 large tablespoons tomato puree
1 clove of garlic, crushed
1 can Tuna in olive oil
Small 50g tin of anchovies
2-3 teaspoons sugar
Black pepper
Big frying pan

As you know I always cook my pasta sauces in a large frying pan as opposed to a saucepan. Much better. Anyway, get everything ready to hand, and start by pouring a big splash of olive oil into your pan, and adding the crushed garlic. Stir that for a couple of seconds, then add the passata. It will hiss, bubble and splash, so a trusty apron is always a good idea! Next add the puree, give that a good stir, then the tuna (drained of most of the oil) and next the anchovies, adding the oil they came in too, sugar and a little black pepper. You'll notice that the anchovies completely melt into the sauce as you're stirring, and they, of course, add the salt.

Turn the heat down to a slow simmer, stirring now and then to gather any loveliness that's collected round the sides of the pan, and cook for about 20 minutes or so. You must taste, and add a little more sugar should you feel it needs it. Sometimes, when it's finished cooking, I like to drizzle a little more olive oil over the top. I know it may sound like a lot, but this sauce seems to love it. Once your sauce is made, it can be left for hours if you like, it will only get better. To make the pasta, either Fusilli or Penne, simply fill a huge saucepan full of boiling water, cook for required time, drain, add a nice knob of butter, and stir into your lovely sauce.

Dinners, picnics and lunchboxes everywhere, enjoy!

BONITO DEL NORTE

ORTIZ

El Velero

EN ESCABECHE

354512

APPLEBATH

FOR THIS DELICIOUS BATH YOU WILL NEED:

Philosophy Apple Bubble Bath, absolutely loads poured
under running water

2 Rub A Dub bath tablets
(available to buy from Amazon)

4-6 cold crisp Washington Red Apples, quartered, served
in a glass bowl atop a bed of crushed ice

Large selection of Church candles, any and all sizes

Tall pitcher of ice cold Cider

...And should you want to make it an Apple Pie bath...
Simply add oodles of Philosophy Cinnamon
Bubble Bath, along with the Apple, requiring only a
gentle swirl with your fingers to mix
beautifully, and
2 fragrant Cinnamon sticks.

*And quite frankly my Dears, should you
choose, as I think would be perfect, to eat
a warm apple pie whilst bathing –*

Well Good For You! xx

Little Lamb Chops

My children absolutely LOVE this, and my Dad, who is all man, thinks these chops are the best thing ever. I must agree. Because in this recipe we are going to use baby racks of lamb and cut them into little chops, they are so so tender, and can be finished in just one bite!

With these little darlings I find it really doesn't matter if you've made too many, as they are simply delicious cold the next day....

Feeds 4 (or several tired, hungry, famished kids)
3-4 racks of lamb
4 fluid oz of Kikkoman Teriyaki marinade
4 fluid oz olive oil
2 tablespoons Dijon mustard
2 large lemons
Roughly 4-5 sprigs of fresh thyme (can use oregano as alternative)
Black pepper
Salt (Maldon sea salt)

You can buy your little racks at the supermarket or butcher, but if you go to a butcher, ask him to trim the bones for you. Right, the first thing you want to do is to cut the racks into little chops. Now don't freak out, you don't need a degree in butchering skills, just a sharp knife! Lay the rack on a chopping board, and if you look you'll see that in between each bone there is a little gap to put your knife. Cut down between each bone, and you'll be left with little chops. Once done, take a rolling pin or something to flatten, give the chops a little bash. Don't go hell for leather and start taking out your frustrations on this poor innocent chop, you just want to smack it a couple of times on the bum safe in the knowledge that it won't phone some helpline...

Put the chops in a large dish, and then make the marinade which later will become a lovely gravy/sauce...

To make the marinade is so easy. Simply weigh out the Teriyaki and olive oil and pour it over the chops. Squeeze over the lemon juice (doesn't matter if the odd pip goes in), add the 2 tablespoons of Dijon, throw in the thyme and lots of black pepper. No salt yet! As with all meats, salt only goes on just before you cook it. Now get your hands in, and mix the whole lot together, massaging and rubbing until everything is nicely combined. You really should taste at this point too.

Cover, and if I'm going to cook it that night, I usually leave it out of the fridge. Seems to take on flavours better.

When you're ready to cook, and bear in mind these guys take literally minutes, heat up a large griddle pan, or large frying pan (if you don't have a griddle pan, you really MUST get one. You'll be amazed at how often you'll use it). OK, so get that pan HOT HOT HOT, and when smoking, put your little chops on. Now don't forget you need to salt the chops, so sprinkle over a little lovely Maldon sea salt, the ONLY salt I use, and cook for about a minute and a half on each side (if you're worried about over-cooking, just cut into one and see how it's doing, no one will notice, promise).

You may need to do these chops in batches, so put the cooked chops on your serving plate, and when all the chops are cooked, TURN THE HEAT OFF under the pan, and pour the marinade into the frying/griddle pan. It will immediately hiss and bubble, which is good, 'cos you're basically cooking the rawness out of it, and this takes seconds. So almost as soon as you've poured the marinade into the hot pan, you pour it straight back out over the chops. Lovely Jubbly!

This lamb is lovely with any number of salads, and also with rice, but because my children have this so often for their dinner, I serve it with some lovely long stemmed broccoli and noodles (packet I'm afraid, I don't weave them myself), but I must admit, that it's just a lovely combo even for us adults, so don't put any leftovers in the fridge, cos you might just be finishing them off after reading that very quick bedtime story!!

FOR A LOVE TO WORK SOMETIMES IT TAKES THIS

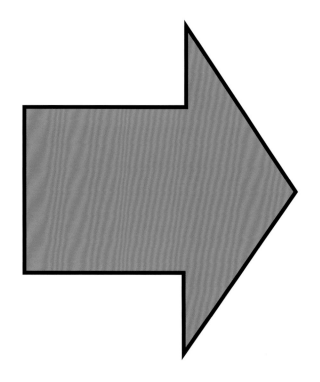

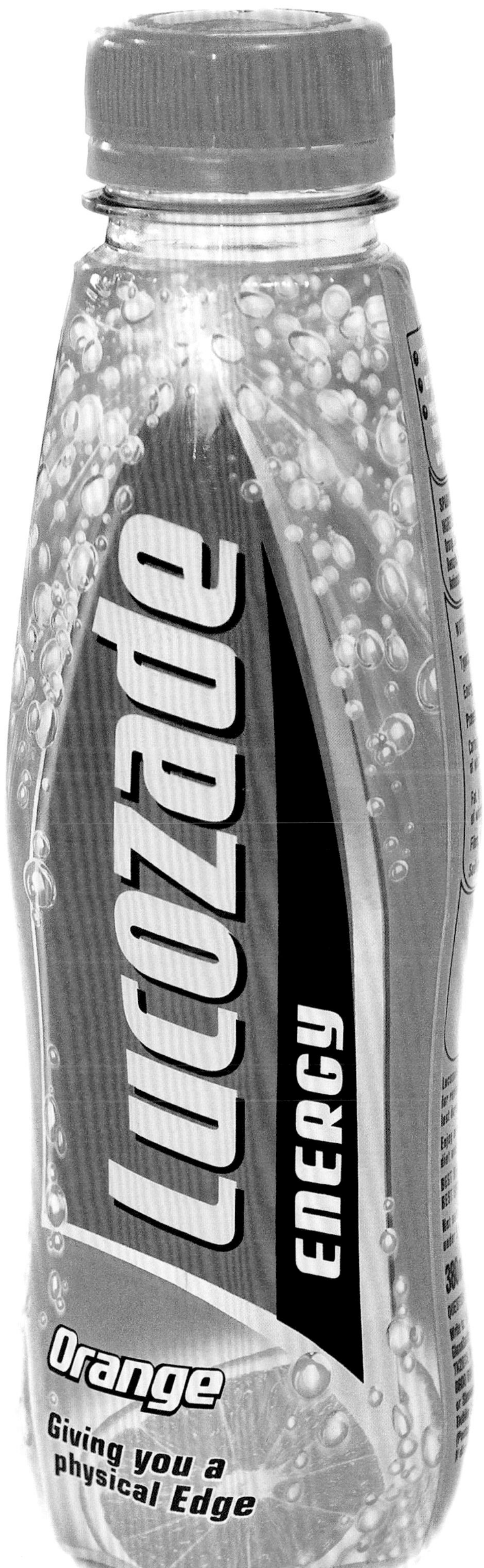
Lucozade
ENERGY
Orange
Giving you a
physical Edge

Romano Peppers with

The other day while in Notting Hill, I ordered a takeaway coffee from a truly beautiful café, and while waiting, this marvellous chef kept bringing out all these wonderful great big dishes, filled with the most gorgeous-looking food. I think it was the artist in me that drew my eye to the dish with the bright red peppers, the golden olive oil, the pure white feta, and those beautiful green

Feta Cheese

Here's how it's done:

5 large Romano Peppers

200gms good Greek Feta Cheese

Couple of vines of Cherry Tomatoes

Couple sprigs of thyme

Small bunch Flat Leaf Parsley

Olive Oil

Salt

Pepper

parsley leaves… Needless to say, I simply had to try to make it, so stealing another blatant stare at this fantastic assembly of health and colour, I raced home to make it…

THE RESULT WAS NOT ONLY REALLY SIMPLE TO RECREATE, BUT MADE UTTERLY WONDERFUL EATING!

PRE HEAT YOUR OVEN TO 190°C/375°F/GAS MARK 5

With a sharp knife, cut the peppers lengthways, top to bottom, but try to also cut through the green stem. Although you won't be eating the stem, it looks so rustic and lovely, it's a shame to cut it away. Place the cut peppers in a small roasting tray. Next, halve the cherry tomatoes, and throw them into the tray as well.

Pull the leaves off the thyme sprigs, and scatter them over the peppers and tomatoes, and throw the whole de-leafed sprig in too, for extra flavour.

Now, drizzle a lovely olive oil all over, add lots of salt and pepper, and put in the pre-heated oven for 15 to 20 minutes. We don't really want the peppers to go all soft and mushy, it's so much fresher to have that lovely bit of bite, but we do want them to just 'soften' slightly, and at the same time, the tomatoes to soften gently too, so the juices from both merge and mix together... Mmmm

When the time is up, take the oven tray out of the oven, and transfer the peppers and tomatoes to a beautiful large serving dish, making absolutely sure you get every last bit of juice out of that oven tray! This is all that wonderful flavour you just made, so please, take your time, it's worth it. xx

Then cut the feta into small cubes, and scatter over the peppers. At this point, it's nice to 'accidentally on purpose' crumble a few of those feta cubes. Gives it that natural, rustic beauty.

Roughly chop up the parsley, and throw that over, and finally drizzle with a little more olive oil.

Simple, rustic, beautiful.

Filling a House

Your home is like your soul, your essence, the essence of you.

Surely you would do the very best for its image, more than image, its 'feeling', the very 'feel' of the place.

You may fuss and say that to make a room *beautiful* costs money, and it's easy to do if you have money, and not so easy if you don't, and you would be **right, and wrong,** on both counts.

To make a room look beautiful, the pieces you put into it must be beautiful to you... If all you can afford is an old wooden chair, then just think how beautiful Van Gogh made that look. For many years now, people have stared at this simple image, and yet, it is its simplicity that makes it beautiful.

So if all you can buy is this lovely old wooden chair, then paint the walls for the chair, strip the floors for the chair... And in this instance, the world can keep its gold and cut glass, for nothing could be more lovely next to your chair than an old jam jar filled with daisies.

PISSALADIERE

THIS IS A **PROVENCAL TART** MADE WITH **ONIONS** AND **TOMATOES**, AND I HAVE TO TELL YOU IT **TASTES ABSOLUTELY WONDERFUL.** PACKED WITH FLAVOUR, IT'S A GREAT STARTER, SERVED AS JUST A LITTLE SQUARE ON A PLATE AS IT REALLY GETS THE TASTE BUDS GOING...

...THOUGH ADMITTEDLY,

I HAVE SERVED JUST THIS TART WITH A GREEN SALAD FOR WHAT WAS SUPPOSED TO BE A 'LIGHT' DINNER, AND WE ENDED UP DAMN NEAR FINISHING THE WHOLE THING...

TASTY OR WHAT!

12 CHERRY TOMATOES
1 CLOVE GARLIC
1 SMALL ONION, FINELY CHOPPED

3 LARGE SLICED ONIONS
BUTTER
½ TUBE SUN DRIED TOMATO PASTE
¾ TUBE TOMATO PUREE (LARGE SIZE TUBE, OR 1 WHOLE SMALL)
TEASPOON OR SO OF SUGAR
OLIVE OIL
SALT AND PEPPER
BLACK OLIVES, PITTED, ABOUT A HANDFUL OR SO
ROUGHLY 12 ANCHOVIES

1 PACKET OF READY ROLL SHORTCRUST PASTRY
(OUT OF ITS BOX AND AT ROOM TEMP.)

FRYING PAN
HEAVY LARGE SAUCEPAN
ROLLING PIN
BAKING SHEET

Now for some reason I start by making the topping in 2 separate pans. I guess you could throw it all into one, but this is how I do it, and as I'm of the mind 'if it ain't broken, don't fix it' I have always done it this way. First take your lovely sweet cherry tomatoes, and slice them in half, and chop the small onion finely. Glug a nice bit of olive oil into a frying pan, add the tomatoes, onion, and squeeze in the garlic… Toss that around the pan till all is soft and lovely, add a little salt and pepper, then turn off the heat and set aside.

Now for the large onions: Get a lovely big heavy saucepan, and add a hefty splash of olive oil, and a generous dollop of butter… once the butter is foaming, add the large sliced onions, and turn the heat down to low/medium and cover. What you are aiming to do here is slowly cook the onions till they are meltingly soft. This will take between 15 and 20 minutes of watching and stirring, making sure the onions don't colour and stick, but just cook down beautifully… when all is soft and tender, add the cooked tomatoes to your onions and stir in. Next, add the purees and sugar, and taste for seasoning. At this point I like to add a lovely splash of olive oil too… Keep stirring this gorgeous mixture around till you have what looks almost like a marmalade chutney. Turn off the heat, and leave to cool to room temperature.

Pre heat the oven to 200°C/400°F/Gas Mark 6

Take your pastry and unroll it. Then with your trusty rolling pin, roll the pastry to a large square/rectangle, remembering that rustic is the name of the game here, so perfection is out of the question.

Transfer the pastry to the baking sheet (do this by rolling the pastry around the rolling pin, then Unroll onto the baking sheet). Once you have your pastry sitting pretty on the baking sheet, take your fingers and gently 'crimp' and curl up the very edge of the pastry. This just acts like a lip and also looks good once cooked.

Now take your beautiful Provencal mixture, and spread it over the top of the pastry, right up to the lip. You may have a little of the mixture left over, and I'm sorry about that, but I don't know how to write it for less.

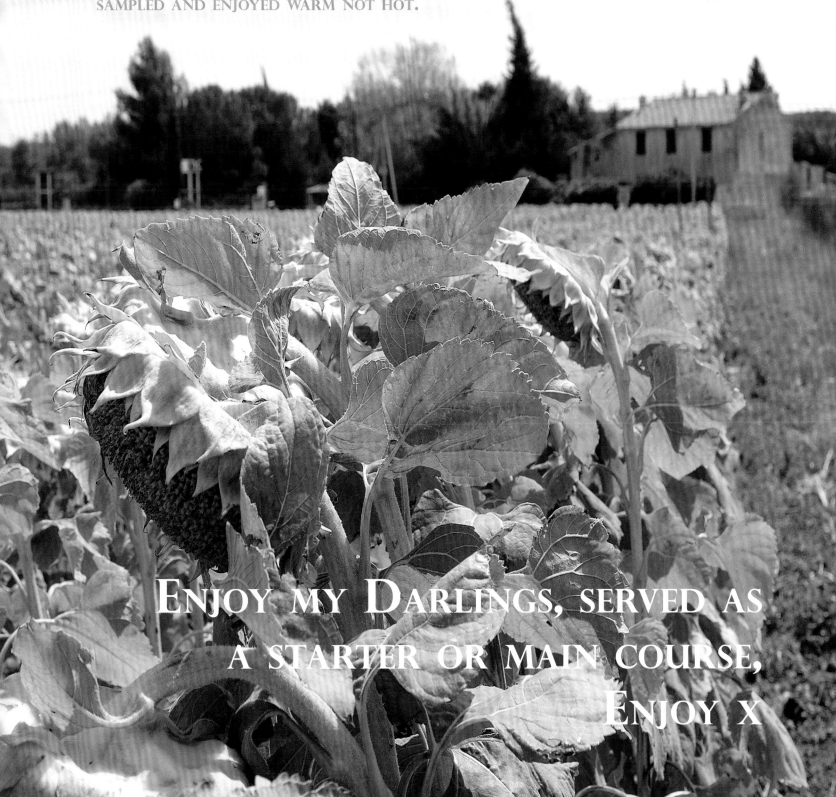

Anyway, once you've spread the Italian and French countryside over the pastry, you now add the anchovies and the olives, making sure that each slice will receive one of each, then simply put the tart into the oven for roughly 40 minutes, keeping your eye on it toward the end making sure it colours beautifully, but does not catch and blacken too much.

When time's up, remove the tart, and leave to cool on a rack before serving, and all these magnificent flavours can, and indeed must, be sampled and enjoyed warm not hot.

Enjoy my Darlings, served as a starter or main course,

Enjoy x

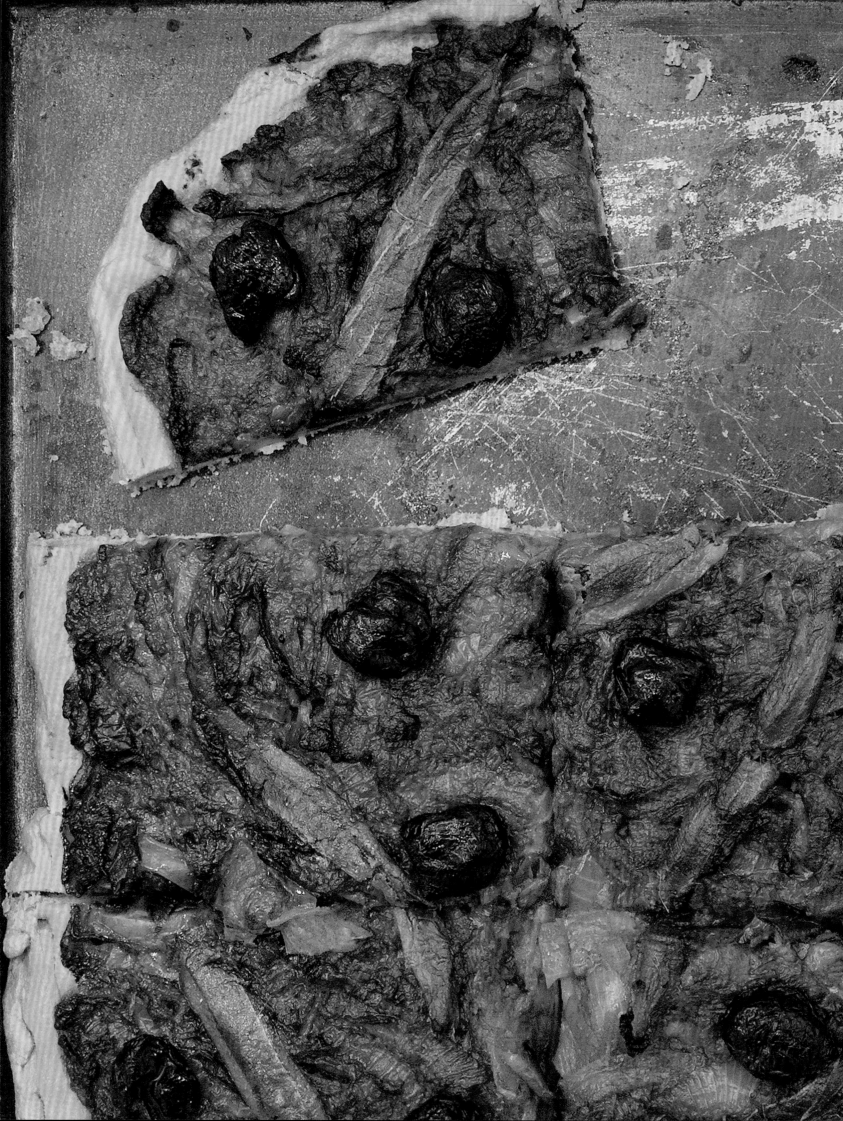

Wedding Salmon

The wonderful Jamie Oliver made life so much easier when he started this great
concept of an entire dinner in an oven tray,
(at least I think it was him... he has my vote anyway)
This is one of his recipes,
except I've added asparagus tips.

Also, I don't know why, but whenever I eat this, I always think of wedding food.
Maybe if you serve this to your unsuspecting fella, he might
think of weddings too... you never know ya luck!

Serves 4 (or a not so hungry 6)
6 salmon fillets
2 packets (200gms) of asparagus tips
1½ packets (250gms) French beans
2 packs of cherry tomatoes
2 tins anchovies in olive oil (100gms)
Juice of 2 lemons, plus extra for squeezing over after
Olive oil
Salt
Pepper
Pre heat the oven to 180°c/350°f/Gas Mark 4

Ready for how easy this is...

Take a large oven tray, throw in the beans, asparagus tips and tomatoes. Place
the salmon on the top, and season the whole lot with salt and pepper. Then
squeeze over the lemon juice, a couple of lugs of olive oil, get your hands in,
and mix it all around, making sure all the ingredients are coated. Next, add
the anchovies. I like to put one or two on each piece of salmon, and a few
over the beans, but hey, I'll leave the artistic licence to you.

That's it!

In the oven for about 20/30 minutes or so, and it's ready to serve!
(Though I must admit, I like to leave the tray sitting for a
little while so it cools slightly. Don't know why, but it seems
to taste better warm as opposed to scorching hot).
Either way, when you're ready to serve, give the tray another
squeeze of lemon juice, and a little more olive oil. Lovely.

I CAN HEAR THOSE WEDDING BELLS NOW!

Love Eachother. Try for one another. Care. Be kind. Laugh when you thought you didn't have laughter in you. Cry with Eachother. Sing. Touch when it's hardest, Touch when it's rejected, Touch again. Be strong. Be soft. Be honest, but forget. Never forget. Fight, Debate, But above all talk. Hold tightly. Hold loosely. Be brave, Be scared, and show both. See happiness. Believe in magic. Marvel at nature, Stay in awe of life. Eat together, Dance together. Adore your memories. Dream and Believe, Dream and Believe. Don't hope, Know. Explore, learn and listen. Stay Home. Keep safe. Honour and respect what you have.

Love is a gift, don't even throw the paper away.

SMILE

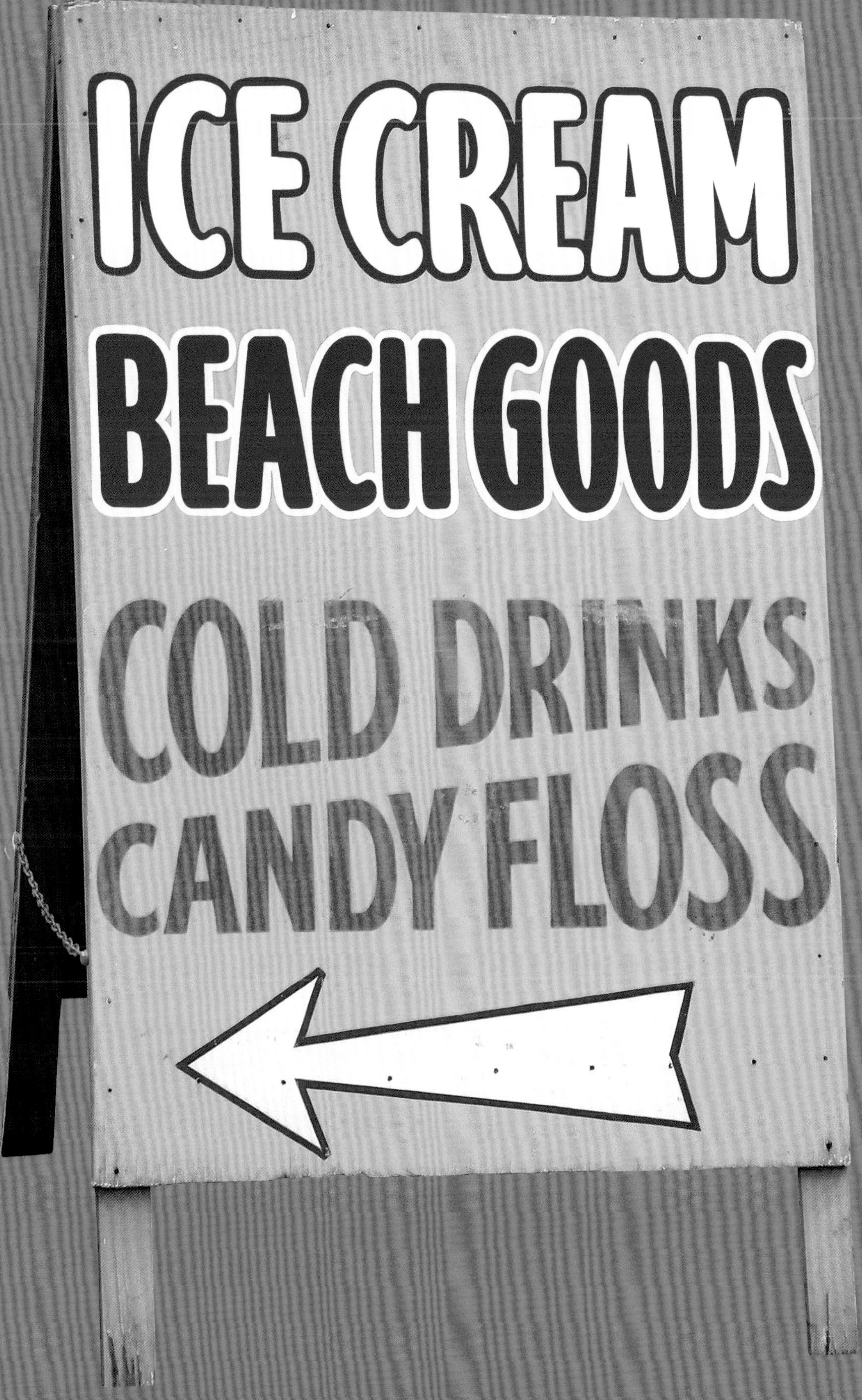
ICE CREAM
BEACH GOODS
COLD DRINKS
CANDY FLOSS

Fruit
Salad
Syrup

OK, this is wonderful. Really people, it's beautiful stuff, lasts forever and it can be used for fruit salad, or as a syrup for a cocktail, with or without the alcohol… It is also one of the most beautiful things you can make. It looks so pretty, and tastes even better. Completely changes an ordinary fruit salad into something really special. Dinner parties, breakfast, drinks, it is a must-have in the fridge, because everyone will use and love it.

And it's this easy....

1 pint of water
350gms/12oz caster sugar
Zest of 2 lemons and juice
Zest of 2 oranges and juice
1 cinnamon stick
1 fresh vanilla pod

Pour the water into a saucepan and add the sugar. Next, using a zester, zest the oranges and lemons into the saucepan. Then with beautifully perfumed fingers, place a sieve over the saucepan, and squeeze the juice from the oranges and lemons. Throw in the cinnamon stick. Now with your vanilla pod, I want you to think of it as something very special, because it is. This is real vanilla guys, not some nasty fake, but the real deal.

Lay the pod on a flat surface, and with a sharp knife cut carefully down the length of the pod. Now inside are all the precious little seeds, and that's what we are after, so using your knife, gently scrape down the pod, collecting as many seeds as you can, but without scraping down too hard onto the skin of the pod. Put the seeds into the saucepan, and throw in the empty pod too cos it's loaded with flavour. Please now just smell your hands... and if you see a loved one walking past, you really must stop them, and hold their face in your hands and kiss them. A citrus vanilla kiss... x

Place the saucepan over the heat and bring it to simmering point, stirring to dissolve the sugar. Then, turn the heat off, and just leave it there to cool down, giving all those wonderful ingredients a chance to become one truly beautiful syrup. Now, like I said, this syrup can be used in a variety of ways, but for a fruit salad you can use any type of fruit, just chopped up and put in a pretty bowl, with a little, or a lot, of the syrup poured over. I would, though, add any soft fruit – i.e. strawberries – at the last minute.

If you did just want to just use berries, and this is my personal favourite, simply arrange them on individual plates, spoon over a little syrup, add a dollop of crème fraiche or double cream if you prefer, on the side, and a little sprig of mint... Perfectly lovely. x

...and

butter

5-Hour Slow Baked Leg of Lamb with Butternut Squash

I'm sure there are many versions of this slow baked lamb, but this combination of tender, fall-off-the-bone lamb and sweetness of the butternut squash totally does it for me. It has such a wonderful stew-like quality about it, but at the same time the leg of lamb keeps its shape, to which our lovely men folk can simply pull pieces off, smother in gravy, and tuck in with the help of a big hunk of bread... Filling, warming and guaranteed to leave your man rubbing his tummy and happily grinning from ear to ear.
X

Serves 4-6
2-2½kg leg of lamb
4 large red onions
1½ butternut squash
3 potatoes
4 or 5 large carrots
8 streaky bacon rashers
Few sprigs of thyme
Couple bay leaves
1 bottle dry white wine
1 bottle water
3 lamb stock cubes

Beautiful crusty loaf of bread – you choose what type

Oven tray for browning
Deep-sided oven tray for cooking
Tin foil

Pre heat the oven to 180°C/350°F/Gas Mark 4

Right, now the hardest thing you'll have to do is brown the lamb and vegetables... So really not that hard at all, and for such little work, you'll get such massive reward. It is a good idea, as always, to have all your vegetables ready to throw into the oven tray (in case you're wondering why I'm using an oven tray to brown, it's because it's much bigger than a frying pan, and just gets the job done quicker). So before you start browning, top and tail the carrots, and cut in half, peel and quarter the onions, and quarter the potatoes (no need to peel). The butternut squash can be a complete bast**d to peel and chop, but SO worth it. You'll also have to scrape the seeds out too, but that's no big deal.

Once done, take the large metal oven tray (have the deep-sided one ready to hand too), pour in some olive oil, and place it over the heat. Salt and pepper your lamb, and into the hot tray it goes. Use a fish slice and a two-pronged fork as you're browning your lamb, or you'll never be able to turn it. Throw in as many vegetables and as much bacon as you can get into the tray too, and brown them as well. Thyme and bay leaves can go in too. Keep turning the lamb, and do the same for the vegetables, placing the nicely browned ones in the deep oven tray as you go.

If the tray starts to look a little dry, just add a little splash more olive oil. It will take you about 15 to 20 minutes to brown all the vegetables, bacon and lamb, but will make the end product look and taste fantastic. Your deep-sided oven tray should be packed full by the end of all that browning, and looking pretty damn tasty already.

Now with the wine, which you'll be adding next, turn the heat off under the oven tray, and pour in the whole bottle of white wine and watch it bubble away, collecting all those lovely bits that would otherwise have been left behind. Carefully pick up the tray, and pour over the lamb etc. Next, fill the same wine bottle with water, and pour that over too. Throw in your stock cubes, and then cover the whole thing with tin foil. Paranoia actually becomes a good thing now, because you really do need to wrap it well, making sure there are no cracks or holes anywhere.

Carefully lift – I say carefully 'cos if you do what I did once and pick it up too fast you end up with half the gravy on the floor! So carefully lift and place it gently in the oven. Close the door, dust your hands off and smile, because that's practically it! So go happily about your afternoon knowing your gonna have a very well fed and happy man in about 5 hours' time.

Your kitchen will smell so wonderful as this starts to cook, and if you do decide you want to have a little look-see halfway through, maybe turn the lamb, taste the gravy, that's cool, but just please be careful when moving it for reasons I explained before, and also PLEASE remember that when you lift up that foil the steam is gonna be bloody hot, so for goodness sake, don't burn yourself! Still, now you know the hazards, it's worth doing.

When the 5 hours are up, and this is another reason why I love this so much, simply turn off the oven, and leave the lamb, still covered, inside, till you're ready to serve. There really is no major time limit on how long you can leave it for either, I've left it for up to an hour before, and it's still been wonderfully warm; in fact, much nicer warm than piping hot which just burns your mouth... So when you're just about ready to eat, warm the bread in the oven, get your man to pour you a lovely glass of red wine, transfer the lamb, vegetables, and all the beautiful gravy to the biggest serving dish you have, walk proudly to the table, and enjoy the whole hearty lamb, bread and wine experience...
I know he will.

Bathing is not simply about cleansing,

It's about immersing, forgetting, enjoyment…
warmth, calmer breath.

It's about, thinking … pondering … solitude.

It's about sharing, talking, laughing;
Clearing the air, and filling it with scented steam.

The BIG Cafe Fry Up

THE FRY UP, BETTER YET, LIKE AN EAST END CAFE ON THE CORNER FRY UP.

Nothing fancy, nothing poncy, just a good fry up. Big mug of tea, fried eggs, bacon, sausage, toast and Brown or Red.

OK, SO THERE'S A POSSIBILITY OF BEANS, OR MUSHROOMS, AND IF YOU WANT EITHER, COOL, JUST A LITTLE EXTRA WORK WITH THE TIMINGS AND YOU GOT IT, BUT I HONESTLY BELIEVE THAT, FOR THE PURPOSE OF THIS, EVERYONE WILL DO JUST FINE WITH OR WITHOUT.

Serves 5 to 50 depending on manpower and pans

PACK OF WALLS SAUSAGES

PACK OF CHIPOLATA OR SKINNIER SAUSAGES

2 PACKS OF STREAKY BACON

SLICED LOAF WHITE BREAD

PAT OF ANCHOR BUTTER

LOADS OF EGGS

2 BIG FRYING PANS

OVEN TRAY

BIG SERVING PLATES

KETCHUP

HP BROWN SAUCE

TEA

I've made bacon and eggs often, as I'm sure we all have at some point in our lives – for the kids' dinner, for mates, etc, but one of my best times to make this is on a Sunday when it's just me, my kids and my man.

Sunday is a special day for the reason that it's a real family day – a day that starts with the boys playing football, whatever the weather, and the girls in charge of baking a cake, music on, singing along to all those songs girls love to sing along to, the boys arriving back with flushed faces and mud-covered knees, the 5-minute lull before the resounding shout of "Lunch is ready!!" and the pounding on the stairs that follows... But most important is the eating together – passing round the brown sauce, talking, listening, sometimes all talking at once, and sometimes mouths too full to talk, for a moment, at all. But together. And even if the whole episode takes but half an hour, because the football, or rugby or whatever is on, go with it, that half hour is still something that belongs to all of you as a family. And that's what counts.

Right, now are we ready, 'cos with this you gotta be, and that's not at all because it's hard to make, it's just timing. So – 2 big frying pans, one on the heat, and the oven turned to 'warming', so, low. Inside the oven, an oven tray waiting...

First start with the sausages in the pan. Now I feel I must tell you that when I asked my Dad once many many moons ago should you stick a fork in a sausage before cooking, he replied 'only a prick pricks a sausage'... Ah, my Daddy and his words of wisdom; needless to say, I've NEVER since pricked a sausage.

Right, so sausages into hot frying pan. I don't see the need for oil or butter in a non-stick pan. Keep shaking the pan, this way and that, like a big ol' café owner, and when they are starting to get nice and brown, turn the heat down a little under them, and put the second frying pan on to the heat. Keep on shaking the pan with the sausages in, and in between doing that, lay the bacon strips into the second pan. Your sausages will be almost there now, so after another minute or till you're happy with them, transfer them to the warm oven tray, and put the sausages in the oven and the frying pan back on the heat ready for more bacon.

Now, while this is going on, you are, of course, keeping half an eye on the second frying pan with the bacon, pressing down occasionally with your fish slice.

Into the sausage pan go more strips of bacon, by which time if you haven't already turned over the first batch of bacon, then I suggest you do it now! Keep frying your way through 2 packs of bacon, placing the cooked bacon on a piece of kitchen roll before you throw it into the oven with the sausages… (by the way, your pans have been on the heat for a long time now, so you can cook on a low/medium heat as opposed to high – you want to crisp, but not burn).

When the bacon is cooked and in the warming oven with the sausages, throw the pans straight into the sink, and rinse with hot water, then without burning yourself, rub dry with kitchen roll.

Now, the toast. If you can grab someone to do this when you're at the end of cooking your bacon, great. If not, then you do it now. It's just a matter of copious amounts of white bread into a toaster, buttered to the edges, thrown into the warming oven as soon as. Get the kettle boiling, and make sure that the tea pot is full of hot water to keep warm, whilst you wait for the toast, as well as sugar and milk (in a jug please) on the table.

Eggs next. When the toast is done and in the warming oven, heat both frying pans and add a knob of butter to both. Crack 4 or 5 eggs into the foaming butter, trying your best not to break any yolks! Eggs will take a couple of minutes, so now's the time to shout for everyone to come sit…

As soon as the eggs are cooked, carefully with a fish slice transfer them all to one huge plate (looks amazing), pile the toast on another, serve the sausage and bacon on another huge plate, or straight from the oven tray.

Take everything to the table, pour big mugs of tea, and get stuck in!!

BUNNY

Best Carrot Cake Ever !

This cake really is as the title says, and as Carrot Cake is one of my absolute favourites, I should know! I would even go so far as to say it's actually dangerous to have sitting around if you're a lover like me, as it's totally IMPOSSIBLE to stop eating!

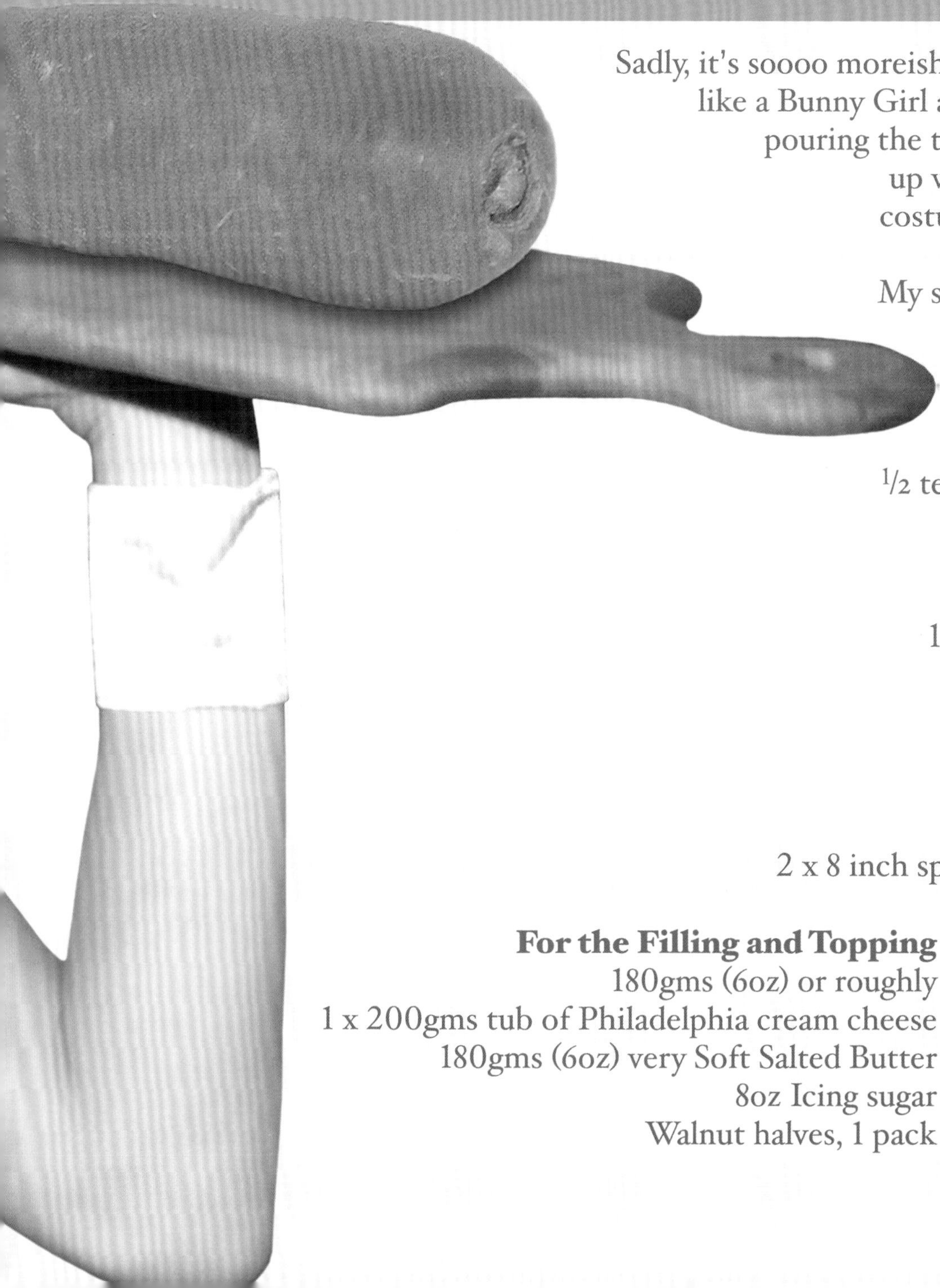

Sadly, it's soooo moreish that the sexy idea of dressing like a Bunny Girl and seductively pouting whilst pouring the tea and feeding the slices, ends up with the great 'Big' Bunny Girl costume feeling really rather tight:

My suggestion, just wear the heels!

250gms self-raising flour
170gms muscovado sugar
170gms soft brown sugar
1/2 teaspoon freshly grated nutmeg

3 teaspoons cinnamon
1 teaspoon mixed all spice
1 teaspoon bicarbonate of soda
75gms dessicated coconut
300gms grated carrots
3 large eggs
175ml sunflower oil

2 x 8 inch spring loose bottom baking tins
Big mixing bowl
Cooling rack
Cake stand
Pallet Knife

For the Filling and Topping
180gms (6oz) or roughly
1 x 200gms tub of Philadelphia cream cheese
180gms (6oz) very Soft Salted Butter
8oz Icing sugar
Walnut halves, 1 pack

Pre heat your oven to
150°C/300°F/Gas Mark 2

Another reason why I love this cake so much is that although there are a lot of ingredients, it's ever so easy to make, and really quite beautiful BECAUSE of the ingredients...

Start by rubbing butter all around the inside of your tins, then take about a tablespoon or so of flour, and sprinkle the inside of the tins. Give them a shake and a turn and a pat here and there, and you end up with beautifully coated tins.

Take a lovely BIG mixing bowl, and start by sifting the flour into it. Once that's done, add the sugars (watch how they move in the bowl... magic!) and then add the cinnamon, nutmeg, all spice and bicarbonate of soda.

Now, get your hands in there and give the whole thing a good mix, perfuming the air and breaking up any lumps of sugar. (This is important because you don't want to find lumps of sugar in your cake after it's baked, so keep shaking your bowl, watching as the lumps come up to the surface, and then crumble them with your fingers. Keep doing this till you're satisfied.)

Next, add the coconut, and stir that in.

Now comes the hard bit, when I say hard, I mean the hardest part of making this fabulous cake, which is grating the carrots! Hardly back-breaking labour, but still, enough to feel it in your arms and with the amount you'll be eating, any form of pre-workout is good! I find it's best to grate over a plate, and also for quickness and arm cramp's sake, grate the carrot on its side, as opposed to its lengh.

Once that's done, add to your big bowl of delights.

Next, and finally, fill your measuring jug with the required amount of oil, add the 3 eggs, give it a little stir to break the eggs up, and then, using your fingers, simply make a little well in the centre of your mixture, and pour in the oil and eggs.

Now it's just a question of mixing, and mixing and tasting... who could resist tasting... and mixing...

Divide the mixture as evenly as you can between the two cake tins, without giving yourself too much grief as to whether you've been exact, just do your best, and put into the oven, close the door, and wait for an hour, or just under if you have a really fast oven...

Meanwhile, make the filling/topping.

Now, I have to admit, this is actually DOUBLE the amount a normal human making a normal cake would use, but I am not part of that race, and remembering that this is a "Sexy Sexy Bunny" and Britney "Gimme Gimme" cake, I simply HAD to give it the required debauchery it so deserves... So I did.

Mix the cream cheese, butter and sugar in a bowl, I find a firm spatula is good for mixing, although I'm sure a wooden spoon would suffice, beat nicely, and again, once mixed, taste… Mmmm, how naughty is that!!

Once your cakes are cooked, the top feeling springy to the touch, remove them from the tins and leave to cool on a rack. (And I do mean leave to cool. I've been so impatient on several occasions that I've iced before the cake was cool, thus melting the icing and had to keep pushing the top half of the cake back on because the bloody thing kept sliding off... Icing was everywhere and I was totally covered BEFORE the sex kitten event. Funny, but not good.)

So once cool, we ice. Now, don't get too worried or hung up on the exactness of this. I promise it will work out just fine. Take a lovely big dollop of the icing and spread all over the flat side of one of the cake halves, and spread right up to the edges. Take the second half of the cake, and place it on top of the iced half. There you have your filling.

Place the cake on the cake stand, then put another big dollop on top of the cake, and using your pallet knife, spread all over the cake. The sides are the hardest, but not so hard that you can't do it, just hard that you may have a little more finger licking to do, which really is not such a bad thing. Just keep on playing with your trusty pallet knife, using it this way and that to get the sides all nicely covered, and any leftover icing just gets added to the top.

When all the icing is done, and you're feeling very proud of yourself for a) not eating all the icing, and b) making it look so lovely, add the walnut halves to the top of the cake, making sure that each slice will be served with a juicy nut atop!

ENJOY WITH A CUP O'TEA, A SEXY MAN,
AND THE BEST 4 INCH HEELS YOU'VE GOT!

Strawberry Pavlova

*Created for **prima** ballerina Anna Pavlova…*
*Delicate, **light as a feather,** and oh so **beautiful** to look at.*
I think this was one of the first things I ever made. It looks
so impressive, but unlike being a ballerina, it's really quite easy.

Serves 6

4 large egg whites

8oz caster sugar

½ lemon

Rock salt

2 Punnets of large strawberries

Large tub, about 200 fluid oz double cream

Mint leaves

Anna Pavlova - Prima Ballerina
12th February 1881 - 23rd January 1931

Pre heat the oven to 150°C/300°F/Gas Mark 2

Line a baking sheet with grease-proof paper. Get some kitchen roll and rub some soft butter all over the paper to be extra sure there's no sticking.

Now take a large bowl and sprinkle in some rock salt. Get your half lemon and rub the salt around the bowl with it. This totally gets rid of any grease, which egg whites absolutely detest! So make sure that bowl is squeaky clean!

Rinse the bowl in cold water, and dry. You should be left with a bowl that looks like it's come straight out of an advert. Weigh out the sugar and place a dish cloth under the mixing bowl so it doesn't slide around.

OK, you're ready to start. Break your egg whites into the bowl, being careful not to break the yolks after all that cleaning. It's really annoying if you do, so if you don't feel too confident about it, break the eggs into a separate bowl then just pour in the whites. Start beating your whites (**I use electric beaters because it's quicker, but a large hand whisk is groovy too**). You'll see they start to turn white and lots of wonderful bubbles start to appear. Keep beating till when you turn off the beater, you can form a sort of soft peak. Then, little by little, start to add the sugar – the mixture should end up very white and beautifully glossy. Apparently if you've done this right, you should be able to turn the bowl upside-down and the mixture should stay there… **Do ya feel lucky? Well, do ya…?**

Take a spatula and pour the mixture onto the oven tray, but don't spread it too thinly; it should be roughly 8 inches wide and a couple of inches high.

Carefully put it in the oven, and cook for about an hour, checking after about 45 minutes. It should be slightly cracked, and sound 'dry' when you tap it. Delia leaves her pavlova to dry out completely in the oven, but I'm far too impatient to do that, but do be careful when you transfer it to a serving plate – **a nice big one** – use a pallet knife to help you. Don't worry too much if you get a few more cracks, it gives it a lovely homemade look, and anyway, you're going to hide the middle cracks with the cream.

Prepare the strawberries by cutting off the top, then standing them on the side you've just cut off and slice top to bottom. You should get about 4 or 5 slices per strawberry depending on how big they are. Beat the cream till it just holds its shape – and I mean just – then again using your spatula, carefully spread the cream on the cooled pavlova, taking it to just about the edge. Take the sliced strawberries and start placing them at the edge of the cream. Keep going all the way round. Once you've done one circle, keep going till you've covered the whole pavlova. Sounds laborious I know, but it really doesn't take that long, and the results are well worth it! Artistically place a few mint leaves here and there, and there you have it – a beautiful Strawberry Pavlova!

P.S. You don't have to use strawberries; raspberries are lovely too, or any kind of summer fruit really.

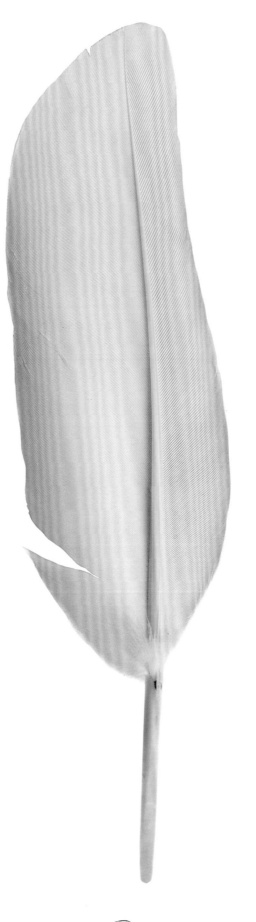

As much as we can

Angels

I refuse to believe that after Biblical times, Angels ceased to appear.
Why would these beautiful creatures simply vanish…?
Could it not be that they did not vanish at all?
Could it not be that we ourselves may have seen an Angel? Felt one?
Our books now tell us stories of people touched by evil, of shivers down our spine,
of going all cold, but surely for every one side there is another, particularly when
it comes to Good and Bad, as without them, we have no fundamental sides, no coin.

So haven't you ever got a warm feeling from someone, even a total stranger?
Perhaps you've sat feeling sad one day, and someone walked past you,
and took in your eyes, and simply smiled, yet in that smile offered you so
much comfort and understanding that it filled you with a strength to go on.
And though our children are so special, each and every new-born baby
is unique and beautiful. At one time you may hold a baby in your arms,
and you may not even be a baby person, but you stop, because it captures you,
something about its eyes, something so deeply good and pure and magic, that you know
this child was born for a purpose, and the purpose was good.

Perhaps an Angel has walked past you in the street, perhaps by chance,
or maybe for a reason you do not yet know. Perhaps an Angel has actually kissed you;
Maybe just once, but that kiss will remain sweet in your heart forever.
I wonder if an Angel ever fell in Love with a Mortal? It must have happened,
who can say it can't? Perhaps some people have something
in them that was passed down from that Love affair,
and what a beautiful Love that must have been;
Perhaps, some people are part Angels.

think bad, we can think Good xx

Typically French Green Salad

This salad always reminds me of sitting in a little French bistro eating steak, chips, green salad and watching the world go by. If you've never experienced it, then this salad is a little taste of it...

Serves 4

Lovely fresh green salad leaves

Handful of walnuts

1 teaspoon Dijon mustard

2 tablespoons white wine vinegar

Squeeze of lemon

Olive oil

Salt

Pepper

First empty the salad leaves into your serving bowl, and sprinkle the walnuts on top. Now to make the dressing. Take a small bowl and into it put the teaspoon of mustard. Add the salt and pepper, and mix with a fork. Next add a little squeeze of lemon and the vinegar, and mix again. Now pour in the olive oil, it's about six tablespoons, but you can add more or less if you want. It's supposed to be roughly one part vinegar, three parts oil, but rely on your taste buds, and never worry if you feel you have to add more or less of something. As soon as the dressing is made, pour it over the salad, and give it a good toss around. Like I said, wonderful with steak and chips, but also goes great with roast chicken or lamb chops. Vive La France!!

...oooh la la

Pasta Pomadoro

After spending a truly romantic week in the Tuscan hills of Umbria in Italy, and eating some really superb food – those Italians sure know how to eat – this simple pasta still remains one of my favourites. It's just a basic tomato sauce, but so delicious. It's also a fantastic sauce to learn how to make, as it can be used as a base sauce too.

The thing I love about the Italian way of cooking is that there is barely any fuss or complications. Yes, some things are harder to make than others, but on the whole, a few simple ingredients are all you need… but because of this very fact, use the best of those ingredients you can find. Remember, olive oil is very important, as is the tomato passata, which is pre-sieved tomatoes. Also, I try to avoid tins, and go for cartons or failing that, jars. To me, it tastes better.

Do not buy passata that has got any herb or garlic flavour, ever.

Why would you when you can simply add your own, as much or as little as you like…

Now another very important thing I must tell you is this:

Make this sauce in a
LARGE FRYING PAN,
and NOT in a saucepan.

Trust me people, this makes a huge difference. If you think about it logically though, it makes great sense. Instead of trying to cook your sauce from the 'bottom up' so to speak, your sauce is distributed across a larger heated surface, therefore cooking and thickening up much quicker, as it will take much less time for any unwanted liquid to evaporate.

SERVES 2

OK, so we start. You'll need:

1 large frying pan

Garlic crusher

1 carton Passata sauce

½ clove of Garlic

½ a tube of tomato puree

Olive oil

Salt

Couple of teaspoons of sugar

Couple of sprigs of fresh Basil
(stem included as this is where all the flavour is)

Black Pepper

Parmesan Cheese
(a good block of it, not nasty pre-grated stuff)

½ Packet of Linguine Pasta,
or Spaghetti

Turn the heat on under your frying pan. Pour in a generous splash of olive oil, and then squeeze in the garlic, using the garlic crusher, and cook that for a second or two, but don't let it burn. Next add the passata, give that a good stir, and then in goes the puree, and again, stir. Should smell just **gorgeously Italian** right about now… Now add a good pinch of salt, the sugar, a little black pepper and basil (no need to chop the basil up, just throw it in whole, stem and all).

Now all you do is let that simmer away on a medium/low heat for anywhere between 15 to 25 minutes, stirring occasionally so it doesn't catch on the bottom. One thing though, after about 10 minutes of cooking, you'll notice that a little sauce will collect around the edge of the frying pan. This stuff is major flavour, so when you're stirring, be sure to add this **flavoursome collection** back into your sauce. The beauty doing of this is that not only have you just added flavour, but given the edge of the pan room to collect more…

Taste your sauce whilst it is cooking, always, to see if it needs any more salt, sugar or even a drizzle of olive oil, but please do make sure that when you taste it, you blow on the sauce first to cool it down. I stress this for two reasons: firstly, if your sauce is too hot you will not be able to taste it to see if it needs anything, and secondly, if you don't listen and burn your tongue, you won't be able to **enjoy the finished product**, and believe me that would be a great shame…

Right, now during the time your pasta sauce is cooking, you can fill a **large saucepan** with hot water and put it on to boil, ready for the pasta. But don't start to cook your pasta till the sauce is ready, still sitting in the warm frying pan it was cooked in, covered if you like with a little foil, or just left waiting…

Do not add the pasta till your water is boiling. Not just simmering guys, boiling. When boiling, add a good pinch of salt and a splash of olive oil. Cook your pasta for the required time, then drain in a colander.

What I do next is very un-Italian, but it's something I have always done. Basically, after draining the pasta, I put it back into the saucepan, then add a knob of butter and toss it in. It just seems to give the pasta a lovely richness, and you know how I love to **break a few rules**…

Anyhow, that done, take your cooked pasta, and add it to the warm sauce in the frying pan, and gently stir it around till the pasta is coated with your beautiful sauce. Next, take your big block of **Parmesan cheese**, and grate a nice amount into the pasta, and toss it through. More is added to the top of the pasta at the table.

I actually serve this straight from the frying pan, beautifully rustic, and of course this way you can be very Italian and use a lovely hunk of bread to rub round the edges of the pan gathering any leftover sauce…

a note to girls…

if you break the

Cinderella Rule

too often, you'll end up looking
like one of the ugly sisters…
even your feet will grow, and
those twinkly shoes won't fit.

Love your Sleep,
Stay Beautiful
X

Lazy Slow Roast Sunday Lunch Lamb Shanks with Creamy Mash Potato

I wanted to find a Sunday lunch that felt like a Sunday lunch, but one that didn't take all morning – and afternoon – in the kitchen.

Roast beef and Yorkshire pudding is always gonna be a winner, but I think this is pretty damn good too! It's lovely on a cold wintry day, as it's so soft, it's almost a stew.

Just remember we are using lamb shanks which for some odd reason seem to always be sold frozen. So either order them from your butcher defrosted a few days in advance, or defrost the night before, otherwise there will be total panic in your kitchen on Sunday morning, and this is absolutely NOT the intention of the Lazy Slow Roast!

4/6 lamb shanks
6 medium size carrots, chopped in half
2 large onions, peeled and quartered
14 fluid oz red wine
8 fluid oz water
2 lamb stock cubes
Couple of bay leaves
Couple of sprigs fresh thyme
1½ teaspoons sugar
Salt
Pepper

For the gravy you'll need roughly a tablespoon of flour, and roughly the same of butter mixed into a paste.

Mash potatoes
8-10 Maris piper potatoes
Butter
Milk
Double cream

First thing Sunday morning… well I say first, but first thing just has to be a lovely cup of tea, so second thing Sunday morning, around 9ish, pre-heat your oven to 150ºC/310ºF/Gas Mark 2, then brown the lamb. To do this, simply take the biggest saucepan you have, splash in some olive oil, salt and pepper the shanks, and brown them over quite a high heat, turning occasionally. While that's browning, take a deep-sided oven tray and pour in the wine and water. Add the carrots, onions, herbs, sugar and stock cubes. It shouldn't take long to do this, but keep an eye on the lamb so it doesn't burn.

Once the lamb is lovely and brown, put the shanks in the oven tray with the wine. Next cover with tin foil, and make sure all the sides are nicely sealed. Put into the oven (time should be roughly 9.30ish), and that's it!! Now you can relax, read the papers, go back to bed and watch an old black and white movie, re-runs of *Little House on the Prairie*, or whatever. You can baste and check on the lamb occasionally through the morning, but basically it's done.

Now to save even more time, you can also make the mash an hour and a half or so in advance. Peel and half the potatoes, and put in a large saucepan of hot water. Add a hefty pinch of salt and bring to the boil. Cook till the potatoes are all lovely and soft (by this I mean when you stick a knife into one it falls immediately off the knife), should take roughly 25-30 minutes.

Once the potatoes are cooked, drain them in a colander, and leave them to dry.

Take the saucepan you cooked them in and over a low heat, add in about a cup of milk. Just warm the milk through, and then take off the heat. Now put the potatoes back in the saucepan, add a large, and I mean LARGE, chunk of butter, salt and pepper, and to make them really sexy, pour in a little double cream. Then mash mash mash! Taste and add more butter, salt, milk, cream, whatever you feel it needs. There are no real measurements when it comes to pleasure! When you've done with all the mashing, take a little hand blender, if you have one, and give the mash a very quick blitz. I know this is not technically allowed in the cooking world, and using a potato ricer (which is great by the way), or mashing by hand is the way you're supposed to do it, but you know what, I really don't care much for that particular rule, so I'm breaking it, and so long as you don't blitz for more than a couple of seconds (you get wallpaper paste otherwise), then why shouldn't we all have lovely smooth lump free mash?

To keep your mash potato warm, cover the saucepan with a tea towel, and the lid. At around 1.30/1.45 check to see if your lamb is ready. It should be lovely and soft, and practically falling off the bone. If so, transfer the lamb, carrot and onions to a plate, and cover with tin foil to keep warm. Now the last thing you do is make the gravy. Very simple: take the oven tray that you have just removed the lamb from, and place directly over a medium heat.

Next, take the flour and butter paste that you made earlier (sounds very *Blue Peter*, but those guys were so in control) and add to the gravy. Keep stirring, and bubbling away till all the butter and flour paste has dissolved into the gravy. Your gravy will be slightly thicker now, and lovely and shiny, but you really must taste it to see if it needs anything.

Right, all that done, serve individually by putting a lovely amount of mash on the plate, placing a lamb shank on the top, few carrots here and there, and then spoon the gravy all around. Sometimes life just doesn't get better than this!

PS. Remember to put the extra gravy on the table, as inevitably people will want more… And of course, a beautiful bottle of wine to help with the Sunday afternoon sleep! xx

Happiness inspires.
It's a wonderful magic,
a beautiful music.
To find it is to treasure it,
for it's the only way
to keep it.

Pies

Mmm just the word brings out the Homer Simpson in me!

Do you know, I know so many people that just LOVE pies, and never, ever make them. I have to admit, that until only recently, this was me too. The reason, well I guess if I'm honest, is because of the whole 'making pastry' thing. Much as I encourage you to put love and care, and time if needs be, into whatever you do, I find it totally soul-destroying if you've done just that, and worked so hard, and then your pastry goes and lets you down… So I discovered Ready-Made Pastry!

And you know what, I don't feel guilty about using it. Not one bit. I know that I will put all my love and goodness into the filling, and the pastry will be perfect!

Why should you and me miss out on the whole pie-eating experience? And another thing, you tell your man you're making him a pie for dinner, and I guarantee a 'mmmm, pie' or at the very least a large smile… There is something so satisfying and wonderful about making a pie. The Mother in you just comes racing to the surface! I just love it! And once you've got the hang of it, you can make whatever pie you want. You can have your own pie named after you! And not only that, but you can also play around with the leftover bits of pastry, and stick them on top of the pie! You can cut out letters, flowers, hearts (a personal favourite), you can write 'I LOVE YOU', or even 'MARRY ME' if you feel that way inclined and want to get the message across in a wonderful way! Never feel limited with those leftovers, because that little bit of extra time and care goes a long long way. xxx

Saying this, if you do want to make your own pastry, then go for it, you clever little thing you!

MINCE AND ONION PIE...

This particular pie came about after my lovely man and his mate had just polished off the last of a 'Vicky's Chicken Pie' I had made them, and they were talking about having mince and onion pies as kids. Such a dutiful fabulous woman am I, that I tried to find a recipe, and sadly failed. The look of sheer disappointment that crossed their faces was worse than that of an Andrex puppy that's just had his roll taken away, so I took matters into my own hands…

I have to say I was quite impressed at the result. Not only because it really wasn't hard to make, but also because this is the kind of pie that you can cut a sizeable slice out of, and pick it up in your hands to eat. So not only does this work for dinner or lunch, but also great for a picnic or outdoor romance!

You will need:
10-inch loose-bottomed quiche tin
Big bowl

For the pastry:
2 packs of 375gms Short Pastry
(taken out the fridge, and out of its box,
10-20 minutes before using so it's nice and soft)
1 egg, beaten
Little brush for painting the egg onto the pastry
Rice, or baking beans
Baking paper

For the filling:
750gms mince meat
1 large onion
Couple of Bay leaves
Light Oil or unflavoured olive oil
Nice big knob of butter
Pepper
Salt (but added only at the end of cooking the mince!)

Gravy for the filling:
¾ pint just boiled water
¼ pint red wine
2 beef stock cubes
Splash of Worcester sauce
1 tablespoon soft butter
1 tablespoon flour

Before you even start the pie, it's a good idea to take a pint measuring jug, fill three-quarters with just boiled water, add the ¼ pint of wine, throw in the stock cubes, and add a splash of Worcester sauce. Mix the flour and butter together to form a paste in a separate little cup, and set aside for later.

Right, first chop the onion as you would normally, but keep the pieces quite chunky.
Next, take the biggest frying pan you have and put it on the heat. Make sure it's nice and hot before you add a splash of oil, and a knob of butter. As soon as the butter is foaming, add the onions. Keep stirring because you don't want them to burn, but you do want to give them a lovely colour. If you feel they are burning, then turn the heat down, but continue to cook till they are lovely and soft and tanned all over.
Once the onions are cooked, put them into a big bowl, and set aside.

Now the mince. Basically the same process as the onions. Very large frying pan, high heat, and do wait for that heat, it's important. Add the oil and good knob of butter to the pan, and sort of 'sprinkle' over the mince and throw in the bay leaves. It will hiss and splutter fantastically as it hits the pan, but this is cool, exactly what we want. Keep stirring the mince, but not vigorously, because the whole point of this exercise is to get the mince lovely and brown (at the same time though watching that it doesn't stick entirely to the bottom and burn).

Now, while you are cooking your mince you will notice a weird thing starts to happen… the heat seems to escape the pan, and the mince stops browning suddenly, and goes a bit grey, and to be honest, rather unattractive looking. DO NOT DESPAIR! The mince will be beaten! Carry on stirring, but now allow the meat to catch slightly on the bottom of the pan. Keep doing this, and you will notice that any liquid will evaporate, and your mince will start to colour up beautifully! This whole process will take about 15 to 20 minutes. Toward the end of the mince cooking, add the onions and a little salt and pepper, then take off the heat, and transfer mince and onions back to the large bowl.

Now, the gravy. Really people this is easy, so don't panic, and you've already mixed the water wine etc, so all you do is this: put the same pan that you have just cooked the mince in back on the heat, and pour in the water/ wine mix. Again it will bubble and hiss, but this is good because it means it's gathering any lovely bits of mince and onion flavour from the pan that would otherwise have been left there. Stir gently, and add the butter and flour paste. Basically the butter and flour are going to do 2 wonderful jobs: the flour will thicken our beautiful gravy, and the butter will make it lovely and glossy. Keep stirring away (whisk helps) for about 5 minutes or so. The gravy should be nice and syrupy. Pour the gravy into the bowl with the mince and onion, stir, and taste for seasoning. It may not need it, but you must always taste at every stage… Cover and set aside to cool.

Now the pastry. (I'll bet at this point you're bloody grateful you're not making your own!)
Pre-heat the oven to 190°C/375°F/Gas Mark 4. Take your pastry and gently unfold over your tin. Do this quite loosely as you will be pushing the pastry down the sides, and will need some slack (cut me some slack, Jack), but don't worry you can always patch up any little tears or holes with a little leftover scrap once you've cut away any extra pastry from the sides of the tin. Next, prick the bottom of the tin with a fork, put a piece of baking paper over the tin, and pour in the rice (uncooked, but you knew that, right…) or baking beans, and place gently in the oven. Cook, or as they say, "bake blind" for 10 minutes. Once cooked, pick up the edges of the baking paper, and remove paper and rice/beans from the tin.
Let that lovely pastry cool now to room temperature or thereabouts.

Finally, filling the pastry…
Pre-heat oven to 200°C/400°F/Gas Mark 6. Using a large spoon, give the mince and onion mixture a good stir and put mixture into the tin. Press down gently, and generally pack the meat in. Now take your second roll of pastry, and again gently roll over the top of the pie.

Cut away any excess pastry using the side of your knife against the tin, and make a little hole in the centre of the pie with the tip of your knife. And the rest of the decorations or words, my darlings, are up to you. Please play now and have fun… this is the best bit of pie-making!

When you've finished playing, brush a little beaten egg all over the pie, and cook for roughly 30-40 minutes, or until golden brown, and looking really quite marvellous…
To take the pie out of its tin (and give the thing 10 minutes of cooling time before for both your sakes, excited as you may be…) simply stand the tin on a mug, or small bowl, and gently ease the sides off. Then, ever so CAREFULLY, using a palette knife, ease the pie away from the base, and onto a serving plate fitting your magnificent pie!

And you have your pie. Quite simply, as my man would say, marriage material!

Bramley Apple and Cinnamon Pie

Before we start, a confession. I originally made the filling for this pie as an accompaniment for yogurt. You know, like the ones you can buy in a supermarket, yogurt on one side, fruit on the other, a fruit 'compote' if you like, because my man seemed to have developed a passion for them. Anyway, I bought all the ingredients I thought I'd need, and off I set on making it. I thought I'd done a pretty good job, but after serving it to my man, with the yogurt, as intended, he suggested that perhaps it would make a better pie filling! At first I thought, the nerve! But having made an entire saucepan full of the stuff, I chose to gracefully bow to his ever-so-polite suggestion…

Now I know, bless them, that the male species is not often correct, though they do try, but in this case I must humbly admit, if only just this once, that this man was absolutely and entirely correct.

In fact I made 3 pies out of my saucepan-full !!
Here's how:

7 Bramley apples
70gms butter
150gms raisins
105gms light brown sugar
1 tablespoon cinnamon
1 cup of water
600gms of short pastry cut into 3 equal pieces

Firstly, peel the apples. Then slice off around centimetre thick slices – please don't be exact – then cut those slices into little cubes. Place a large sauce pan on the heat, and then add the butter. When the butter has started to melt, throw the apples in, and toss and stir together. Next add the raisins, sugar, water and cinnamon, and stir the whole lot together. Immediately your kitchen air will be perfumed with the beautiful scent of apples and cinnamon. It's honestly worth making for this moment alone... x

Now, cover your saucepan, turn the heat right down, and let this wonderful mixture stew and cook for around 45 minutes to an hour, stirring occasionally. If you think it's looking a little too dry, or sticky, then don't be afraid to add a little more water. Please do taste it too, but be careful not to burn your mouth. When that's finished its cooking, set aside in a separate bowl to cool.

Now the pastry. As you know I shamelessly admit to buying ready made. I love the stuff. But by all means please make you own if you're so inclined. I wanted to make this pie a little different, and looking at the apple and cinnamon mixture, the colours and smells reminded me of skiing, and wintry things, and for that reason the thought of 'wrapping' the mixture in the pastry appealed to me.

So, pre heat the oven to 180ºC/350ºF/Gas Mark 4, then cut the pastry into 3 equal pieces, and roll each piece out to roughly a 10-inch square (do this one piece at a time, covering the remaining pastry with a damp tea towel, or with its wrapper, so it doesn't dry out). Now with your square, cut and steal about an inch or so off the top of the square, to cut shapes out of and use to decorate the top, and set to one side.

Next, spoon about a third of the mixture onto the centre of the pastry square, and carefully with your spoon, fashion the mixture into a kind of fat rectangle, leaving about an inch at either side. Sounds complicated, but really it's not, just do it, you'll soon see what I mean. Now what you do is fold the top and bottom end of the pastry OVER the mixture, and then tuck the sides UP towards you. The reason I say up, is because once you've done that, you need to transfer the pie to the oven tray, and flip him over in the process. Don't worry, use your hands and a fish slice to help you and all will be fine.

Next, cut out any shapes or letters with the remaining pastry (I couldn't fit 'wow you were right my clever darling' on mine, so I just did hearts…), and using a little pastry brush and some milk, or beaten egg, brush the pastry all over, then sprinkle with a little caster sugar. Repeat the same with the others, or if it's just the two of you, you can always keep the rest of the mixture for another pie another day, or go ahead and make all 3 and wrap bows around the other two and give them away as fabulous 'Homemade Pie' presents – who doesn't want one of those ?

Either way, cook for around 25 to 30 minutes or until your pie is lovely and golden all over. Take out of the oven, and once transferred to a beautiful serving plate, sprinkle with caster sugar, and serve slices of pie with lashings of cream and cups of tea! xxx

The 'Man with A Cold' Bath

Poor Darling,

Home cold from work, sniffling in his dripping jacket. Brave, brave man, who worked all day long, each and every moment spent battling against this dreaded virus… He really doesn't know how he managed it…

The Strong Silent Male. Well, I say silent, but only about his well-being – everyone and everything else gets barked at… Clearly this red-nosed, sneezing Alpha Male needs gentle handling….

Alert your stations, and slip into action.
Run him a Hot Bath using:

Aromatherapy Essentials
… and be quite generous. It's strong stuff, but it works magic on clearing His head, and taking Him to a better place.

Add a little Dove Crème Bath, because it's so much nicer to sit in a few Bubbles…

NB: Make sure all windows and doors are shut throughout the bath-running, and once the bath has run, turn the shower onto 'HOT' only, and allow the bathroom to really fill up with steam. We are going for the full Turkish Mode here, so steam as much as you are able.

SQUIRE

A GOOD BOYS READ

By the side of the bath leave:

– L'Oreal Face Scrub
– L'Oreal Cleansing Gel
– And also leave a moisturiser for after bathing.

(I have used L'Oreal because my Mr Man likes it, if
yours has a particular favourite then please use that.)

Now, if He needs a shave, and the poor Darling
feels up to it, provide:

- Gentleman's Shaving Kit with Brush and Shaving foam

(if he doesn't have one, use His razor and shaving foam,
making sure both are tidy and fresh looking. The Gentleman's kit
might make a nice present one day…?)

- A mirror, large enough to shave in
- Roll a towel up for Him to rest His weary head

…and finally,

with muted Classical music playing gently in the background,
serve a good inch of Single Malt Whisky in a heavy tumbler
glass…

…either with a splash of Highland Spring Water, or neat…
You know your man, and if you don't, then learn now. x

I hope you feel better soon Darling x

Embrace the Elements...

*So the rain makes your hair go
curly, so what, in fact great,
curls are lovely;
Go with it...*

*And the heat makes it go flat, well then
flat it is. Look upon it as 'sleek'...
Frizzy is a problem, so solve it
with a handful of water.*

*Whatever the weather, if your smile
is wide, and your eyes are happy,
you'll always look great!*

... And that is absolutely true! x

mama burgers!

The hamburger. Better yet, the homemade hamburger. There really is nothing better than picking up one of these and biting into it. Ketchup, mayo and juicy burger all over your chin and hands… With pickles, onions, cheese and bacon, or sour cream and chilli sauce, or even plain, these guys are simply the best!

Makes roughly 10-15 juicy burgers…
1kg mince beef
1 large grated onion
4 tablespoons Tomato Ketchup
2 heaped teaspoons Dijon or English Mustard
4 tablespoons Teriyaki Marinade
1 egg yolk
Pepper
Packs of Burger Buns, cut in half, and both sides spread with butter

Sliced Cheddar Cheese
Grilled Streaky Bacon
Pickles
Sliced Onions
…or whatever you fancy!

Right, first things first. Grate the large onion, then in a little frying pan, add a drop or two of olive oil, and fry the onion till it softens. Set to one side.

Now put the mincemeat into a large mixing bowl, add the egg yolk, ketchup, mustard, pepper and teriyaki, throw in the fried onion, then get your hands in there and mix and squish and mix some more. What you need to do now is shape the burger patties. There are really no rules as to how big or small you can make these guys, they can be tiny little kiddie ones, or big fat boy ones. The best thing to do is to look at the size of the burger bun you're using, and shape accordingly. So, grab a handful of the beef mixture, and squeeze, mould and shape into a large ball. Then pat the ball down into a burger shape, and then gently smack round the sides to neaten it up. Please, though, do not stress and panic if you don't have a perfect circle, you're making homemade burgers, not wedding rings, and there's nothing wrong with them being a little rough round the edges. xx

Once done, put them in the fridge for a couple of hours before cooking because this seems to help them stay together whilst you're cooking them, but again, if you can't, don't worry.

Now to cook them, get a great big frying pan, or even two smaller frying pans, and make sure they are hot hot before you put your burgers on. When they are on, you'll have to keep your eye on them because they go very brown very quickly. So put them on, and watch them sizzle away for a couple of minutes, then turn them over, and at the same time, TURN THE HEAT DOWN under the frying pan. They should only take about 3 to 4 minutes now, and you want to keep then all lovely and juicy, so don't over-cook them!!

Now, if you're having cheese burgers, once you've turned them over in the frying pan is the time to add a couple of slices of cheese on top of each burger. The heat of the pan will melt the cheese even though it's not in direct contact, but what you can also do at this stage, is get a large saucepan lid, and cover the top of the frying pan. This helps to stop them drying out, and melts the cheese quicker.

Once done, take your burger off the heat and onto a plate ready to be made into the best damn burger you ever had…

OK, guys, now it really is up to you what you want to put in your burgers – if you're going to have bacon, though, make sure it's cooked before you make your burgers.

I do have one trick, which I actually discovered by accident, and will probably send chefs screaming out of the kitchen because it involves the dreaded microwave, but hey, I'm not a chef, and neither are you, so we can break all the rules and do what we want! (I must though say that in general I am no lover of the microwave, so don't start thinking it's OK to use it for everything, but in this instance it serves its purpose beautifully).

My trick is this: burger buns. For years I have been making these burgers, and although the burger itself was always mighty tasty, I could never find a way to warm a burger bun without drying it out completely. I tried putting it under the grill, tried toasting, neither worked. Then one day when I was trying to get to my man's heart through his stomach, I told him I'd bring him a takeaway Mama Burger. I wanted it to be warm, so put the whole burger, with cheese and bacon, onions and tomatoes, on a buttered bun, on a plate, covered it with a piece of cling film, and put the whole thing in the microwave for 30 seconds or so….

The bread was warm and meltingly soft, the cheese gooey, the meat juicy… And the man?
Let's just say I still have his heart. xxx

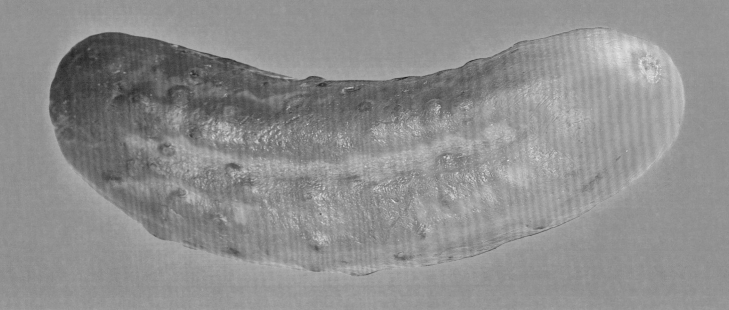

The Forest and Honey Bath

Oh do I LOVE this bath so !

On a cold, dreary, bleak night, it's like slipping into sweet comfort… surrounded by candles, their light, adding, coupling, the warm Honey Glow. Its so good, it takes you back to a childhood world where all was buttery and good. And that's a beautiful place to spend an hour or so

xxx

For this experience you will need…

As many candles as you can: large, small, either, both, all.

Laura Mercier Crème Brulee Honey Bath, absolutely oodles of the stuff, spooned in with that delicious Honey spoon

Cup of hot sweet Tea, or if you prefer, a tall glass of Milk

Hot buttered, and I mean BUTTERED, White Toast, dripping with Clover Honey

And… Enid Blyton's 'The Far Away Tree'

And the flower… well I think for this you need, and you will find, if the season is right, Twisted Willow Branches, and perhaps a little Moss…

But, either and every way, Flowers, Beautiful Woodland Flowers!!!

One of one, a bunch of something else, any and all colours! Bluebells, Daffodils, Hyacinths, Cow Slip, Berries on Branches, Fox Gloves... basically any thing that you can grab that looks like it could have been picked!

Beautiful Magic Wood feeling, and Honey... It so Belongs Outside with the Nature from whence it was Created... The Birds and The Bees... In fact, the perfect thing to do would be to put a little Bird or two on a couple of the branches... How perfectly gorgeous would that look!

Now remember, these baths can be given as Gifts, either to Yourself or to a Loved one... so it's well Worth the Effort.
I know I would love it so much if someone did it for me, made me a Honey Bath...
I would probably cry x

BEAUTIFUL GREEK BUTTERFLY PRAWNS

8 OR 10 TIGER PRAWNS
3 CLOVES GARLIC
4 SPRING ONIONS
JUICE OF 4 LEMONS
HANDFUL OF FLAT LEAF
PARSLEY, CHOPPED
8 FLUID OZ OLIVE OIL
LOADS OF SALT AND PEPPER

This dish is so great for a light dinner. Great too because once you have made the sauce and butterflied the prawns, the cooking time is virtually minutes. I also find the whole 'getting covered in olive oil while eating with your hands' thing kinda romantic…

I first fell in love with these prawns at the tender age of 7 when my family first moved to London… They are from THE best Greek Cypriot restaurant called Halepi, which is as popular today as it was back then! I can remember sitting with my parents, and my brother and I using the prawn shells as little spoons to scoop up this totally wonderful sauce, elbow deep in olive oil and lemon juice… Ah, those were the days I thought, but then I thought, hang on, they can be mine again…

OK, so first you need to buy your prawns. GO TO A FISHMONGER! Firstly, because you simply cannot get these beauties in a supermarket, and secondly, because we simply MUST support these wonderful local businesses. You know I find it ever so sad that we live in a world with our Butcher, Baker and Candlestick maker rapidly disappearing… Supermarkets are great, but these little shops, they are far too special to be missing from our lives. They are what make a high street…

Right, sorry got sidetracked in my cause. Ask your fishmonger for some Tiger prawns, and get him to 'Butterfly' them for you, take the heads off, but for goodness sake, DON'T let him take off the shells or feet. This is a severe crime. I'm not kidding, it's against the rules. You could just as easily buy them whole and do this at home, it's really so easy, you simply cut the heads off (keep them, they make an amazing base for a pasta sauce), hold the prawn firmly in your hand, and with a sharp knife cut down the middle, just splitting it open, and flatten it out. Pull out the little black thing, and you're butterflied!

Once you've done this, put them in the fridge till you're ready to use them.

To make the sauce is very easy. Get yourself a nice size mixing bowl to let your sauce sit in, and begin. Peel and 'bruise' your garlic, by bruise I mean just bash it about a little with the flat of your knife, so that the flavour escapes, throw in your chopped spring onions, parsley, and squeeze in the lemon juice. Go crazy on salt and pepper (remember, ONLY the marvellous Maldon sea salt will do), and then add the olive oil. Mix that all up, and the wonderful smells of the Mediterranean should fill your kitchen… Taste to check for seasoning, and if all is groovy, leave to sit for a couple of hours.

Now to cook them heat up a large griddle pan (if you don't have one, get one – it's the best investment you will ever make), or else, a really large frying pan, perhaps even 2 frying pans if one isn't big enough. Heat the pan/pans up HOT, and I do mean HOT, smokin' HOT. Now whilst the pan is heating, get your prawns, and tip them into the marinade, and using your hands, mix them around in the sauce. Remember, you're gonna be using that marinade to make the sauce at the end, so keep it close to you. I also suggest that you wear an apron whilst cooking this, and tuck a tea towel into your apron to wipe your hands on, and a fish slice and fork to cook with, and a large serving plate at the ready. You'll need it, so do it.

Right, are we ready? Let's go! Take your prawns, and one by one, place them FEET SIDE DOWN next to each other on the hot pan. Press down on each one with the fish slice. It will look and smell incredible right about now, and you may even get the odd flame firing up, but at no point should you panic; flash flames are OK, they're just that, and look spectacular! Now, because the pan was so hot, the prawns will take no time at all to cook, so after about a minute or so, lift up

the prawn you put on first, and if his feet are lovely and brown, almost blackened, turn him over, and do the same with the other guys, and again, press each one down with the fish slice, and this time, sprinkle over a little salt. Again, cooking time is very quick, a couple of minutes, and it's honestly better to very slightly under-cook these beautiful creatures than over-cook them to chewy rubber (which is a crying shame). If you are worried, you need to start believing in yourself more, but in the meantime, take a prawn, and just see that the flesh side has turned white; if it has, groovy, all cooked. Remove the prawns from the pan one by one to the large serving plate, then TURN THE HEAT OFF under the pan, and quickly throw the remaining marinade into the pan, literally for about 4 seconds, then pour over those beautiful prawns…
Hello Greece! We have arrived!!!

Now, I serve this with a very simple cherry tomato and fresh basil salad, and an even more simple rocket salad – just rocket, salt and pepper, little squeeze of lemon juice, and small drizzle of olive oil. Really fabulous, healthy, hands-in delicious!

Foreword to Victorian Lady Bath

The title of this bath is driving me crazy.

At first when the idea bloomed, I thought I must have an image of a beautiful lady... a Lady of Shalott-type image, but without the tragic ending. Can you imagine? Not good to have such a beautiful bath, and have such tragedy attached. Perhaps the Greats, the Legends, Shakespeare, and all his magnificent drama would have surely used that image, but no, I wanted my drama to be a play of Decadence and Beauty. And Wealth. I wanted to give the experience of what it may feel like to have only your Beauty to look after. To have time to brush your hair with a silver brush. To have the swirls of perfumed steam rise up and curl around you. To escape to a place that only the very few have been... you are the Leading Lady in my play. It was written for you.

And so I looked for my image, and as I looked, there she was, this beautiful lady. And when I looked further, I found that she was indeed a Victorian Princess.

And so a title was born.

Now, as you should know, I never just write these baths in the hope that they will work, I couldn't put my name to that. No, I Hubble Bubble Toil and Trouble, and I try my utmost to create an Experience that can be recreated, experienced and enjoyed by you, and, unless I feel I have succeeded, then I will not tell you of my lotions and potions, No Sir, no I will not...

But with this bath, as I thought I had perfected it, I invited my man to bathe with me...

Tragedy then struck my title when as we immerse ourselves into the water... ....'Behold the Naked Lovers!' and suddenly, BANG ! we became Romeo and Juliet.

Amid the starry, starry night, deep blue, the experience of wealth became one of each other, nothing else really mattered. Naked we laughed and played and kissed among the stars.

Romeo and Juliet. Us. We were the words
'with love's light wings did I o'er perch these walls;
For stony limits cannot hold love out:
And what love can do, that dares love attempt'

So, please, if there are any Star-Crossed Lovers out there, please
do experience this bath, not as a Victorian Princess, but as only
Lovers can...

The Victorian Princess
Bluebell and Lavandula Bath

For this you must feel Dreamy, Soft, Feminine, and Beautiful
Enter and become a Lady Mystical, Seductive, Secretive
As you bathe amid the Stars
Become Wealth and Perfume,
and let Perfume and Wealth Become You

~

Diptyque Feulle de Lavande Candle

~

Panhaligon's Bluebell Bath Oil
as much as Decadence allows

~

Penhaligon's Lavandula Bath Oil
just enough to add a subtle perfume

~

Both oils poured under Rushing Hot Water

~

2 Rub A Dub Fizzy Tint Dots
added at the Beginning of Time
(and available online at Amazon)

~

A handful of the Night Sky
in the shape of Silver Stars

And, to amuse bouche, wet the lips,
set the scene and fulfil the role

~

A Box of Fortnum & Mason Dark Chocolate Violet and
Rose Creams

~

Tumbler of Bombay Sapphire Blue Gin…
Poured over Ice Cubes

~

Lavender or Blue Hyacinth Flowers in Vases,
or one in a Beautiful Pot

~

Tea Lights… as many as you can… in vases, in cut
glasses,
in any glasses…

~

The Words of William Wordsworth,
or perhaps if you prefer,
Lord Tennyson, to whisper in your ear

…and one last thing, your most beautiful piece of
Jewellery…
Be it a Necklace, Bracelet, Ring, or all three…
…Though a Tiara would be Magnificent

Once your water has filled your bath, the steam rising
filling the air with bluebells and lavender;
your candles are burning, all of them twinkling,
and they are just about all the light you need,
be Naked, but for your Diamonds,
pour the Gin slowly over the Ice,
and gently place your stars over the blue surface

Then step in…
Relax and bathe,
and as you begin to gather the stars off the surface, and
the ones that have twinkled to the bottom;
The last Stars, the ones that you find
when you thought you had gathered them all…

These Stars, these are your Wish Stars…

I hope you find many x

NB: Dear Ladies, please note it's best to lay
a face cloth over the plughole when draining
your bath to catch any fallen stars x

Granny Bumble's Pancakes

PANCAKES. MMMMM... FOR ME THESE LITTLE BEAUTIES
ARE RIGHT UP THERE WITH GUCCI HANDBAGS.

I remember my brother and I going through stacks of pancakes
covered in golden syrup and double cream when we were kids.
How we didn't get as big as houses I'll never know!

The wonderful thing about pancakes, though, is they still taste just
as good today, so if you haven't had any for a while, well wait no longer!

To make these lovely little things, you'll need:

4oz self-raising flour	¼ teaspoon cream of tartar
½ teaspoon salt	1 egg, lightly beaten
¾oz melted butter	About 3 fluid oz milk

(proper old-fashioned recipe, huh!)

My Dearest Granny Bumble left this earth soon after I wrote this.
Beautiful lady, such a beautiful Lady, forever I will remember you.

...Pancakes

Start by sieving all the dry ingredients into a large mixing bowl, then make a little well in the mixture, and break an egg into the centre. Next melt the butter in the microwave, and pour in half the milk. Now slowly pour the combined butter and milk into the middle of the bowl with the flour and the egg, gently whisking as you do. Keep on mixing till your batter is smooth, then add the rest of the milk.

The pancake mixture should be neither too thick, nor too runny. I think the correct term is 'ribbon' stage, simply meaning that if you play around with it, it leaves a sort of ribbon impression. OK, once you feel your batter is the right consistency, you're ready to start.

Take a large non-stick frying pan, or rub a little butter over an ordinary one, and put the pan on to heat. Once it's hot, take a dessert spoonful of the pancake mixture, and 'tip' the batter off the spoon and into the pan. (I think a dessert spoon gives you a lovely size, but by all means use a bigger spoon if you want a bigger pancake, just remember it gets harder to justify eating 10 or more!). Now watch your pancakes. When little bubbles start to appear on the surface, turn them over. The other side will take no time at all, and they are ready when lovely and golden brown.

As entire cooking process is only a couple of minutes, and you'll probably be able to get about 4 pancakes in the pan at once, place the cooked pancakes between two sheets of kitchen paper until you're ready to serve.

Pancakes American style with crispy bacon and maple syrup,
or the healthier, option with a dusting of icing sugar and fresh fruit...

However you choose to eat them they are yummy, yummy, yummy!

Gita's Kleftico Lamb

My cousin Gita really is a great cook. She lives in Johannesburg with all the rest of my cousins, but her origins are Greek. When I asked her how she would feed a man (and believe me the Greeks know how), she gave me this wonderful recipe.

I know I am always saying how easy it is to cook, so long as you add a little love, but really, this one is so so simple, and what you are left with is this fantastic, beautifully soft lamb that just falls off the bone... gorgeous!

Serves 4
4 lamb shanks
1 glass white wine
1 glass water
Juice of a lemon
Fresh oregano, roughly chopped
Lots of salt and pepper
Tin foil
Large deep-sided oven tray

Before we start, I would like to say that for some reason whenever I have bought lamb shanks, they have always been semi-frozen. So I always buy them the day before I need them (Had to add this because I would hate to think of you going to make this recipe, which I have said is so easy, and is, except the bloody lamb is frozen solid!)

Pre-heat the oven to 150°C/300°F/Gas Mark 2. Ok, first put a large frying pan on to heat. Season the lamb all over, and put it in the hot pan to brown it. You may want to add a little olive oil to the pan. Also, lamb shanks are a bit of a bugger to brown evenly, but do your best to give them a lovely even colour.

Once that's done, transfer the lamb to a deep-sided oven tray. Next, pour over the wine and water, add the lemon juice, and throw over the herbs. A little more salt and pepper at this point wouldn't hurt either.

Now the important bit: cover the entire tray with tin foil, making absolutely sure that it is sealed tight (I use a double layer 'cos I'm the paranoid type). Put the lamb in the oven, shut the door and forget about it for about 4-4½ hours, depending on the size of the shanks.

That's it my darlings.
Serve it on a large plate, covered in the gravy it was cooked in, with some crunchy roast potatoes… and if you're gonna be Greek about it, a lovely Tabouli salad too!

Greek Roast Potatoes

4 or 5 large Baking Potatoes
Olive Oil
Salt
Pepper

Pre-heat oven to a hot 200°C/400°F/Gas Mark 6.
Get a nice big oven tray and pour in enough olive oil to fully coat
the surface. Put the tray in the oven to heat. Peel the potatoes,
then cut them in half, lengthways, then cut them in half lengthways
again, so you have a kinda boat shape. If you feel some are a little
too big, then cut them again. Big saucepan filled with boiling water,
in go the potatoes with a hefty pinch of salt, and boil for around
5-7 minutes, or until when you take one out and scratch
its surface with a fork, it 'fluffs' up.

Drain potatoes into a colander, and shake dry.Then take the
lid from your saucepan, place it over the colander and give the
potatoes a really good shake. Really good. Vigorous. Carefully
remove the hot oven tray, and transfer the potatoes, making sure
you give each one a good coat and toss in the hot oil. They will
take roughly up to an hour, so check on them after 20 minutes, and
turn them this way and that, and add salt and pepper. What I do
at this point is actually take a fish slice and 'crush' a couple of the
potatoes...basically guarantees you those delightful, delicious,
dip-your-hand-in-and-steal crispy little flakes of crunchy potatoes...

Add a bit more salt before serving if you fancy, and don't
forget, ever, to retrieve ALL those crispy bits you made in the
'Love Crush'. x

Tabouli

160gms flat leaf Parsley
Couple Mint Leaves
10 medium Tomatoes
5 Spring Onions
2½ Lemons
5–6 healthy glugs of Olive Oil
Salt
Pepper
2oz Bulgur wheat

Make the Bulgur wheat by simply following instructions on packet, or, just weigh out 2oz, cover with water, bring to the boil, and simmer for roughly 10–15 minutes, or until soft. Drain into a sieve, and run under cold water to cool. Shake off excess water, and set aside.

Chop parsley and put into a large mixing bowl. Shred mint leaves finely and add to parsley. Slice and dice tomatoes as small as you can (no stalk bit, please), chop spring onions, and add tomatoes and onions to the parsley.

In goes the Bulgur wheat.

Now it's a question of salt and pepper (lots of), squeezing lemons, (watching for pips), and glugging in your olive oil... Mix, toss, stir and taste... if you have to add more lemon, salt or oil, then so be it. Don't be afraid, go for flavour.
Let that sit out of the fridge before you serve it.

Don't go down.
Well not for long, you can't afford
the luxury.

Though being down may feel like a
warm comforter, blind,
cossetted you sit in its folds, get up.

Get up.

Because down is a liar.
Down says 'I don't care',
'you don't care';
Down lets time pass
without respect.
It wastes.

GET. UP.

DOWN

PASSION FRUIT AND

Tastes beautiful, feels summery
and looks so pretty too.

My favourite fruit salad.

Serves 4-6
5 large ripe mangos
4 passion fruits
Small handful of mint, finely chopped, save a few
pretty sprigs
Small tub of crème fraiche

I wouldn't recommend making this unless mangos are in
season. If it's freezing cold outside, a fruit salad is not
what you need anyway, but all the same, keep this for
summer, or turn the heat up and pretend, also good!

In saying this, sometimes you do get beautiful mangos
when it's cold, and sometimes it's a lovely little dessert
regardless of the weather. You choose.

Either way, always smell mangos when buying them.
Fruit should smell like the fruit it is. If it does then it
will taste like it should.

No smell, no taste. Got it?

MANGO SALAD

Peel and chop your mangos into cubes, or as close as, and put them in a serving bowl. Next, cut the passion fruits in half, and squeeze the contents over the mango. Throw over the chopped mint, give the whole lot a gentle mix, and you're done.

Just serve with a lovely dollop of crème fraiche on the side, and perhaps a sprig of mint too... why not! Simple and beautiful.

This fruit salad can even sit for a few hours, so you can make it in advance, and keep it cool and fresh in the fridge.

GRANDMA SHIELA'S CHICKEN SOUP WITH KNEIDELS

This recipe is from my beloved Shiela. She has cured me many times, not only with this soup, but with the abundance of love she gives me. She is a very very special lady, a true Grandma, a true mother, and I am privileged enough to call her my friend.

This wonderful tradition of Friday night chicken soup was passed down to her, Booba to Booba. I pass it on to you as she did to me, word for word, action for action. Some things, like Shiela, are just too good to ever try and change.
Best made the day before, or first thing in the morning.

Serves 6
2 legs and a breast of a 'boiler' chicken (available at any Jewish supermarket or deli)
1 onion
About 6 carrots, halved
1 parsnip
1 turnip
2 chicken stock cubes (try to get either 'Thelma' or 'Knorr')
Salt
Pepper
½ tablespoon sugar

Large Jewish Grandma saucepan

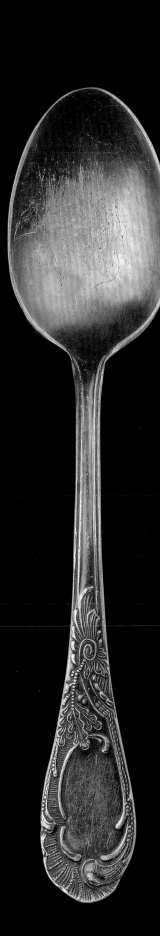

SHIELA'S
REMEDY
CHICKEN
SOUP

SERIAL NO. 37368

Right, like I said, this is her recipe, and I'm not gonna change anything she does, and she does as follows:

First put the chicken in the pot and pour over some freshly boiled water and top up with hot water to fill the pot. Bring that up to the boil, then throw the water away. Yup, you read right, throw the whole lot away, saving the chicken, though, of course. Now, put the chicken back in the pot, and again pour over some boiled water, and top up with hot.

Next add the vegetables. Just throw them in whole, no need to chop up anything. Add the stock cubes, sugar, and season with a pinch of salt and pepper. Bring to the boil, and once boiling turn the heat right down to simmer, cover and forget about it for at least 2 to 3 hours. Read a book, get your nails done, paint the house, whatever...

If you asked Shiela, she'd tell you to just 'schmooze' around. Just forget the soup.

After this time, turn the heat off, and leave the soup to cool. While it's cooling, you will notice that any impurities have floated to the surface, so take a large spoon, and just skim them off the top. When the soup has completely cooled, put it in the fridge.

The next morning, or several hours later, the fat in the soup will have hardened, and will be sitting on the surface. This is called 'schmaltz', and is wonderful spread on a salt beef sandwich. Anyway you don't want it in your soup, so again, using a large spoon just skim it off the top. Then remove all the vegetables, and throw away everything except the carrots, which you slice up, and throw back in the soup. OK, once that's done, either put the soup on to heat, or back in the fridge till you're ready.

These are kinda like a Jewish dumpling. It's the only way I can think to describe them. They are not as stodgy as your regular dumpling, though, and made right, they are much more light and fluffy.

Makes 6/8
1 packet of Matzo meal (available from most supermarkets)
1 egg

You can make these in advance and keep them covered in the fridge till you're ready to use them.

Easy peasy to make. All you do is just pour a packet of matzo meal into a bowl and add the egg. Then combine with a fork, and then, using your hands, pick up a little of the mixture, and roll into a little ball. You should get about 6-8 balls in all.

When you're about 25 minutes away from serving (don't forget to put the soup on to heat), put some boiling water into a saucepan, and add the matzo balls. Cover, and leave for about 18 minutes.

DON'T PEEK!
These are very old rules... are you prepared to go up against a Jewish grandma on her matzo balls? I didn't think so... Anyway, after the 18 minutes, remove your fluffy dumplings from the water, add them to the hot soup, and serve.

My Little Acorns

I am an Oak tree, and around me, our
roots tangled forever, You will grow.

For always I will shade You from the blaze,
and part my leaves for the weakest of light.

I will dig with the very roots of my being
to bring you goodness;

I will drop the little moisture my leaves
hold on to You,
And I will still glisten.

I will grow strong and tall around You,
one step further to the sky than You...

T'would take a mighty axe and days of super
strength to fell me, and still I would remain
deep down, hands in Yours, too strong, too deep,
to ever be parted.

And when You stretch higher than me, Your own
branches thick, I will make way, and become the
richness that feeds.

Marvellous Runny Marmalade

Marmalade is a jam. I know. And I also know you'll think I'm crazy for asking you to attempt to make a jam. I am crazy, yes. I think in life you have to be a little crazy.
But this is no ordinary marmalade...
It's **SO** damn good, and it keeps for ages and ages,
and just think guys you'll be able to say...

"Well actually I make my own Marmalade"

How groovy is that!

What you will need, though, is those cute little jam jars and "homemade" label stickers that you can now use as intended, and not to label whose gameboy is whose!

450gms Oranges

Juice of 1 lemon

1½ litres water

900gms jam sugar

1 plate, "put in the freezer" (just do it, will explain later…)

Now, although this really is not hard, you are making something that will last a long time, and therefore cannot be rushed in the making. Respect this fact, and make this jam on a lazy weekend afternoon, and enjoy the experience. Marmalade is a lovely thing to make, and it will make at least 3 small jars. xx

The first thing you'll need to do is to cut the orange rind off the orange. To do this hold the orange firmly in your hand, and cut the peel in a sort of top to bottom motion, kinda as you would peeling an apple, but not cutting into the flesh of the orange. Try to keep the strips as long as you can too.

Once you've done that, you'll notice the white "pith" on the underside of the skin. This has to go, as it has a bitter and not particularly nice taste. To strip the pith off, place the peeled orange side down, and hold the tip of the peel in your fingertips. Then with a sharp knife, press down on the peel, and with a gentle sawing action, cut the pith away. It may sound complicated, but I would not give you anything that you are not capable of. In fact, the last time I made marmalade, I did it with my little girl... Do make sure you have gotten rid of all the white though. (I suppose you could just use an orange zester, and chance it, but where's the fun in that? Much better to cut by hand.)

Once that's done, lay your peels out, and then cut them into strips. You can make them as wide or thin as you like. Personally, I cut them into really skinny anorexic strips. It's the only time skinny is attractive, and I also like to have as many strips as possible so every serving has got plenty. Once all your orange strips have been cut – and your hands are perfumed with orange oil – put them into a large saucepan.

Add 1½ litres of water to the pan, and then place a sieve over the pan and squeeze the juice from the oranges you've peeled, as well as the juice from a lovely big bouncy lemon. Now place the saucepan over the heat, bring it up to the boil, then turn the heat down and let it simmer for between 1 and 1½ hours, till the water has reduced by half, and the orange strips are tender.

During this time, you really don't need to stand over it, but what you do need to do is occasionally "skim" anything that floats to the surface. To do this is easy enough. Just use a large serving spoon, and gently skim around now and then. I find it best to leave a spoon and a little bowl on the side so it's ready to hand whenever I walk past. When the water has reduced, and all is tender, the real excitement starts, because we are now going to add the sugar!

To do this, you literally tip all the sugar in at once, and gently stir till it's dissolved. This will take under a minute. Then turn the heat up and once it starts to boil, time it for 10 minutes. Any nasties that rise to the surface at this time, just skim away. Please do remember that the contents of your saucepan at this time are going to be seriously bloody HOT, and this is where the plate in the freezer comes in that I mentioned in the ingredients.

While the jam is boiling away, take the plate and stand with it in your hand next to the saucepan. When 10 minutes is up, use a spoon to put a little blob of jam on the plate. Wait a second or two, then with your finger gently give the jam a little push. If it stays runny, give it anywhere between 2 and 10 minutes of boiling, and when it kinda rolls up against itself, much like the skin on a puppy's neck, it's ready. Because the plate is cold, it will help the jam to "set" much quicker, thus giving you an indication of how runny it will be. Clever, huh.

I must say that I love this marmalade really quite runny, hence the name 'runny' in the title, so that when you serve it you do so with a little jam-spoon. Very old fashioned and posh, but why not… When you're happy with the cold plate test, turn the heat off, and let the marmalade stand for 15 to 20 minutes.

Before you put your fantastically lovely marmalade into the jam jars, the jars will need to be sterilised. This really is no big deal. I just pour boiling water into and all over the jars, and then dry the inside with a bit of kitchen roll (clean please), or if they are jars that have contained something else, rinse them thoroughly, and literally boil the jars for 10 minutes.

Finally spoon, or ladle, the marmalade into the jars, God you should be feeling so good right about now… then write your labels and stick them, with great pride, across the front!

Well done, people, you just made your own marmalade. If that's not Housewife and Mother of the Year stuff, then I don't know what is!!!

Spaghetti Bolognaise

Spaghetti

Bolognaise

My babies' absolute best! And I must say I actually don't think I've ever met anyone who doesn't like it. I know I love it, especially covered in ketchup and cheese! Crazy kitten that I am… but hey, don't knock it till you've tried it! Also, I am the world's worst person at freezing things, but I do make **LOADS** of the bolognaise sauce, and freeze it in little 2-portion batches. You never know when your fella might just cancel the party and want a quiet night in… so this way you can be the perfect woman, and say, 'No problem, darling. I'll just rustle something up'…

This amount is for just that purpose, so if you want to make less, just halve the recipe, but remember to taste while cooking, and add more or less of something if you feel the need.
Serves 8
1 ½ kilos minced meat
1 large onion, chopped
2 cartons of sieved tomato
Whole tube of tomato puree
3-4 bay leaves
5 heaped teaspoons sugar
Splash of Worcester sauce
Loadsa salt and pepper
Glass of red wine, if you have any hanging around…
Olive oil
1 packet of pasta – you choose, but spaghetti or penne is always good… or even Rigatoni, my kids go crazy for that !

Right, huge 'Mama's gonna maka you da pasta' saucepan is needed. Add a good few lugs of oil, then throw in the chopped onion. Cook till the onion starts to soften, then add the mince, but not all at once. I normally divide the mince into quarters, wait till the first quarter's cooked, than add the next and so on. It's easier to cook that way, and you want the meat to be COOKED before you add the tomatoes, so be patient and cook it through. If you feel it's looking a little dry at any time, add a little more oil. OK, when that's done, add the tomatoes, and mix through. Next add the puree, I know it sounds, and looks, like a lot, but this amount of meat needs it. Throw in the bay leaves, lots of salt and pepper, Worcester sauce and add the sugar. Sugar? Well the reason it's there is because of all that tinned puree and tomatoes, they just love sugar! Promise, it just works, so do it! At this point you can add the wine, if you have any to hand, and if you've only got one bottle, save it for that dinner. Xxx

Right, turn the heat down really low, cover, but leave a little gap, and cook for at least an hour, stirring now and then, and of course tasting. Remember that this sauce only gets better with time, so make it early if you want and let it sit, or even the day before…

Cook your chosen pasta in plenty of salted boiling water, and when it's ready, drain it into a colander, then put it back into the saucepan. Add a generous knob of butter, and mix in the required amount of sauce… Don't forget the ketchup and cheese and big smiles all round!

It's a Funny Thing

It's a funny thing to witness pain and wholeheartedly
wish it upon yourself;

It's a funny thing to keep shoes that no longer fit,
as though you would a priceless jewel;

It's a funny thing to laugh with tears and swell with pride
at an achievement lost, but sought in earnest;

It's a funny thing that your smile is more important than mine;

It's a funny thing to see innocence, and hear wisdom;

It's a funny thing loving you my children, a funny thing.

Asparagus with Hot Butter

A perfect starter, and one everybody loves…

SERVES 4

ABOUT 3 OR 4 BUNCHES OF
ASPARAGUS, DEPENDING ON HOW
MANY ARE IN A BUNCH AND HOW THICK
THEY ARE
COUPLE OF LARGE TABLESPOONS OF BUTTER
SALT
PEPPER

You have to serve this just after you've made it, but apart from that it's so damn easy…

Fill a saucepan (I use a deep-sided frying pan) with boiling water, and put in on a high heat.

Next, take your asparagus and cut about an inch off the ends. The wonderful Jamie Oliver does this by bending the bottom half of an asparagus till it snaps, leaving you the perfectly edible part only, and I'm sure that is the right way to do it, but patience was never my strong point, so for me it's a large knife, similar to the one used in Psycho, line 'em up, and off go the ends (thank God I'm not a hairdresser right…).

Now add a hefty pinch of salt to the boiling water, and in go the asparagus. They can take between 5 and 10 minutes depending on their thickness, and bear in mind you're going to put them back on the heat once they've been boiled, so don't overcook them. I normally pick one up and gently squeeze the end. It should give a little. (With any vegetable, I always feel it's better to make the mistake of undercooking rather than overcooking. There is nothing less appealing than a mushy tasteless something that once was a vegetable. So when it comes to cooking asparagus, they should be quite soft yes, but I don't think anything wants to end up with the adjective 'droopy' attached to it... asparagus included!)

Once cooked, drain them in a colander, and put the saucepan straight back on the heat.

Take the butter and throw it into the saucepan and let it start to melt for a second or two and start to become lovely and foamy. Then put the asparagus back in, and turn off the heat – any remaining butter will melt. Now go crazy on salt and pepper, shake the pan around gently, so all the asparagus are well coated, and tip the whole lot onto a serving plate, and to the table you go!

PS. If you want to add a bit of sharpness to cut through the butter, a squeeze of lemon over the top does the trick.

SPATCHCOCK CHICKEN with BALSAMIC RED ONIONS

This is just such a great recipe because it's like creating a roast dinner, onions and all, in under an hour! Tender, juicy chicken, and with no bones, it's simply a winner all round. Totally brilliant for an elite dinner party because it can literally be thrown together, thus giving you more time to look absolutely fabulous, calm, cool and collected, and feed your guests the most wonderful food… Your man will walk around with an ear-to-ear grin muttering the words 'What a woman!!'

(What you will need to do, though, is order your chicken from the butcher the day before, because he will need to 'bone' it for you – in other words, remove all the bones except the little wing bones i.e. 'Spatchcock'. You can of course do this yourself, it's really not that hard, and perhaps if I was a more accomplished writer I could talk you through it, but that would probably be harder than boning the actual bird itself!).

Serves 4 hungry, or 6 not so hungry
2 spatchcock chickens
1 tablespoon ground ginger
1 tablespoon crushed dried chillis
8 tablespoons teriyaki marinade (Kikkoman if possible)
Juice of 2 lemons
6 tablespoons of olive oil
3 tablespoons soy sauce
Maldon rock Salt just before cooking

For the Balsamic onions…
4-5 red onions
6 tablespoons balsamic vinegar
Fresh thyme
Olive oil
Salt and pepper

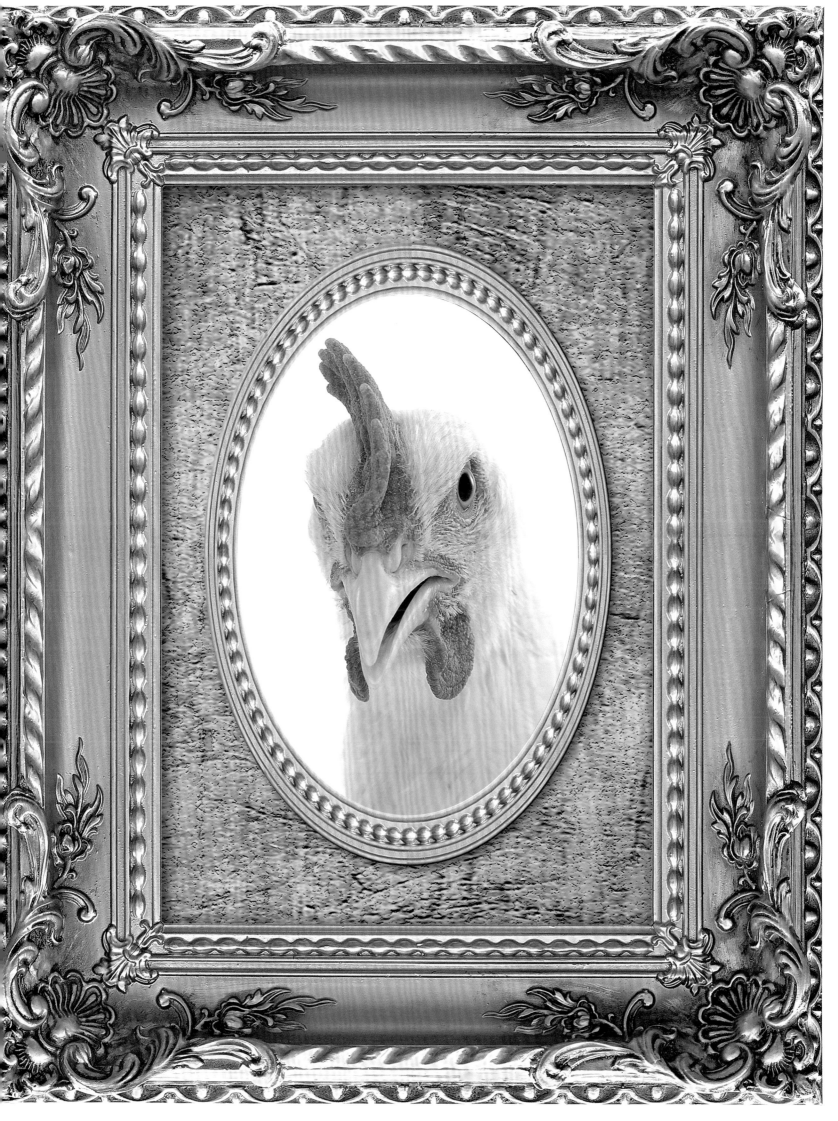

And so we start…

Pre-heat your oven to 230ºC/450ºF/Gas Mark 8.

(I must say though that I never serve this chicken straight from the oven. It really does taste much better when it has cooled down a little, and had time to relax. So you can just leave it sitting warmly, roasting tray covered in tin foil, for up to 40 minutes.)

To start, take your spatchcock chickens, and put them in a large oven tray. Next it's simply a matter of adding all the listed ingredients to the tray, and then getting your hands in and mixing and massaging and more mixing and more massaging. Normally I would tell you to taste the marinade, but as this is chicken, you can't. Inhale deeply instead.

When the massage is over, and the chickens have a feeling of wellbeing about them, arrange it so they both lie flat on the tray, skin side up.

Now for the onions, you just need to peel off the rough outside layer, but leave the root attached. If you hold the onion in your hand and peel downwards toward the root, it makes it easier. I know Nigella says life is too short to peel an onion, and sometimes I totally agree, but life's also too short not to care, and as you're cooking for your family and friends, peeling an onion is really no hardship.

So when you have peeled away the outer layer, cut the onion into quarters, top to bottom, through the root, so that you have a kind of 'mini fan' of onion. Please don't worry though if one or two of them fall apart slightly, as such is life, and we too may occasionally fall apart, but still taste good. x

Put the onion fans into a separate tray, and tuck a few sprigs of thyme under a layer of onion. Then, spoon the balsamic vinegar over each onion quarter, drizzle with olive oil, and add lots of salt and pepper.

The chicken and the onions go into a hot oven at the same time (don't forget to add salt to the chicken before roasting) for roughly 25 minutes. If you're at all worried, just take the chicken out and cut into a chubby part to make sure it's cooked, but as there are no bones in it, it should be just fine.

When all is cooked, transfer the onions to the chicken tray, and serve all together, either in the tray, or on one lovely large serving plate. Great with a lovely crisp green salad… What a woman indeed!!!

Hot Chocolate Sauce for Ice Cream

OK PEOPLE, THIS BABY IS BAD!

THE SEXIEST, NAUGHTIEST SAUCE IN THE LAND...

SO IT'S PROBABLY BEST EATEN IN BED!
Sweet, Melting Hot Chocolate... Cold Ice Cream...
as The Sauce Meets The Cream It Goes
ALL HARD... Rude Enough For You?!?

8oz of dark Toblerone Chocolate
5oz of butter
About a cup full of chopped pecans or hazelnuts

Break the chocolate into pieces and melt very very gently in a heavy saucepan. When the chocolate has almost melted, add the butter. It looks like a lot of butter because it IS a lot of butter, so you'd better start thinking how you're gonna be working that off... (I did tell you this baby was BAD!). So stir that butter into the chocolate till it all comes together (easy now), take off the heat, then add the nuts...

This sauce needs to be served hot, so pour it over the ice cream as soon as you've closed the bedroom door!

Good thing is though, you can keep it in the fridge and gently reheat it when you want it again, rather, if you can manage it again!!

An Appeal

Should anyone out there know of any shop, market stall,
church fair, ANYWHERE that I could buy a Magic Wand,
I would be eternally grateful.
I know that they stopped the sale of these wonderful
magical items after people began to use them in wrong ways,
in anger, for financial self-gain etc, and slowly, slowly,
because of these facts, and a few more too sad to mention,
wands began to disappear.

But I know, I KNOW, there must still be a few out there,
the last few remaining....
I hereby promise wholeheartedly to only
use my wand as it should be used:

For WONDER!
For BEAUTY!
For HAPPINESS!

…and if I do on occasion turn small noisy children, and sometimes large noisy men into cute little woodland creatures, I solemnly promise to turn them back. Eventually.
No, really I will.
I was kidding. Bad timing.
I really really do want a Wand, so please, please, seriously, if you can help, please do so.

Many Thanks,

Stash x

BM BUTTERFLY
LONDON
WC1N 3XX

20 Minute Lamb

We are talking pretty literally here, which is a very good thing if your man decides to tell you at the 11th hour he is bringing the Boss and Mrs Boss home for dinner…

Now for this lamb you will need all the usual suspects for the marinade, which will then become a lovely gravy… You literally start this lamb 20 minutes before you serve, so have everything else ready. If you are making salads, then dress the avocado and tomato, but not the green till the last minute. I have served this many times without potatoes or rice, but if you like, throw a few sweet potatoes in a moderate oven as soon as and before anything as they take a couple of hours, and serve them with lashings of butter! Have your strawberries all ready in pretty little bowls, and cream gently whipped.

Remember, you are an organised and totally in-control Super Woman x

Serves 3-4

3 or 4 baby racks of Lamb

4 fluid ounces Kikkoman Teriyaki Marinade

2 tablespoons Dijon Mustard

3 fluid oz Olive Oil

1½ to 2 juicy lemons

Couple sprigs of thyme, or rosemary or even oregano

Black pepper

Little salt just before cooking

Right, now it's called
20 minute lamb
because it takes roughly
5 to brown, 10 in the oven,
and the all-important
5 to sit.

Pre-heat your oven to 200°C/400°F/Gas Mark 6.
Make the marinade in a large, flat dish so your lamb can sit pretty in it.
Make sure you really give them a good Swedish massage, and even a little prick with a fork here and there to really let those flavours sink in. When you're ready to start, and your oven is nice and hot, make sure you have a smallish oven tray also hot in your oven ready to receive these little lambs.

Pre-heat a large frying pan, and when it's smoking hot, place your lamb racks in the pan, and allow them to brown up nicely, but watch them … 5 minutes or so later, take the hot oven tray out of the oven, put the racks in, and pour over the marinade…

Into the oven it goes, for 10 minutes.

After the 10 is up (don't panic, I know it does not seem a lot, but it is just right, these are only little guys), take the lamb out, and what I do is place the racks straight onto a lovely chopping board, and spoon a little gravy over each one, and pour the rest of the gravy into a sauce boat should needs be.

Now LEAVE them to settle for 5 minutes, call your guests to the table, and present your lovely lamb on the chopping board, and proceed to carve the racks at the table.

BaaBaaBaa! x

NB Working with 0.375kg (max) lambs

Macaroni Music

So called because I know a few lovely musicians that like nothing more than a quick, easy carb fix at the end of a long hard session! I also know that my man and my kids would stand on their heads and sing 'Dixie' if I said it was the way to get Macaroni for dinner! For me, well I guess I would sing too!

2 heaped tablespoons salted butter
3 tablespoons flour, plain or self raising
1¼ pints full cream milk, room temp if possible
6oz hard cheese, grated (e.g. cheddar)
Salt
Pepper
400gms Penne pasta, roughly half a packet

Please note before we start, that you will be using 4oz of the cheese in the sauce, and 2oz sprinkled over the top. This is a roughty toughty measurement so grate and divide without too much worry.

Start with the sauce. As usual have everything but the pasta to hand, including a whisk! Put a medium-size saucepan over the heat, and throw in the butter. Keep stirring till it has all but melted, then put in the tablespoons of flour. As soon you add the flour, keep, keep, keep stirring. The mixture will go all sandy looking and bubble away, but this is good. After about a small minute, turn down the heat a bit, and add about a quarter of the milk. Keep stirring and DO NOT PANIC if the mixture looks totally hideous. Get your whisk, add about half the remaining milk and keep stirring quite vigorously. Keep adding the milk, about a quarter at a time.

Your sauce should look quite runny now, and perhaps still have the odd lump or two. This is cool, people, just keep stirring and turn the heat up, bringing it slowly to the boil, and any lumps will soon disappear. You'll notice that once it starts to boil, the sauce will thicken. Allow it to boil for a minute or so, stirring hard all the time, this time with your wooden spoon (when I say stirring hard, I mean don't pussy foot around, get the spoon in there and stir, all around the sides not just gently in the middle. Think 'buxom') Take off the heat. Right, now what you should be left with is a basic white sauce. You can add pepper at this point, but no salt till you've tasted the cheese, as some cheeses are saltier than others. So do the mouse thing, and taste the cheese! Then all you do is put the grated cheese into the sauce, and this time you stir loving and gentle. The cheese will melt beautifully, giving you a lovely cheese sauce. Now taste the sauce, and see if it needs a little salt. Then cover and set aside while you cook the pasta.

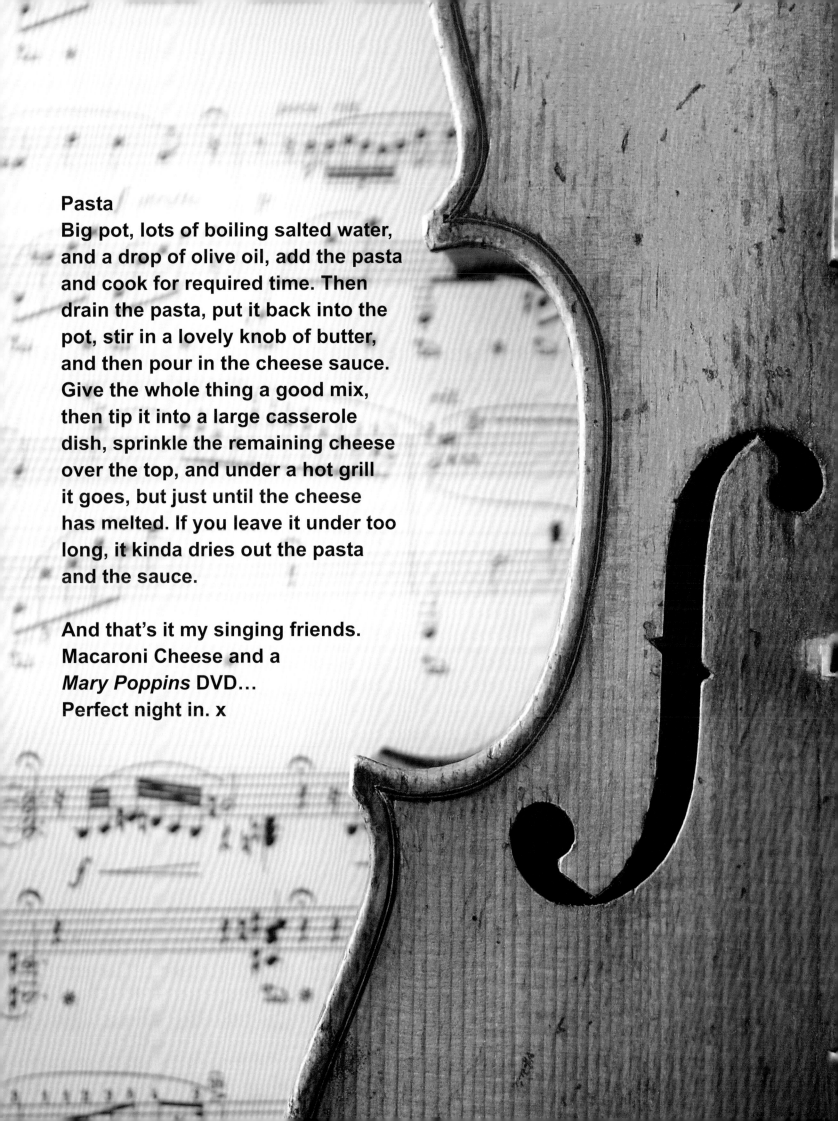

Pasta
Big pot, lots of boiling salted water,
and a drop of olive oil, add the pasta
and cook for required time. Then
drain the pasta, put it back into the
pot, stir in a lovely knob of butter,
and then pour in the cheese sauce.
Give the whole thing a good mix,
then tip it into a large casserole
dish, sprinkle the remaining cheese
over the top, and under a hot grill
it goes, but just until the cheese
has melted. If you leave it under too
long, it kinda dries out the pasta
and the sauce.

And that's it my singing friends.
Macaroni Cheese and a
Mary Poppins DVD…
Perfect night in. x

WHEN ASKED THE QUESTION

**"Do you turn Green in anger,
like the Hulk"**

I Replied

"No, Green is for Envy"

- And I Thought -

Ugly, Sick kinda Green,
I pictured A Grey Green, a Nasty Pale Dead Green,

A really quite Horrid Putrid Green – and it struck me then and
there, I did not want to feel Envy, I do not want to be any of
those shades of Green…

**… And so I will Wish, head tipped,
and Sincerely, Well.**

Aunty Alma's Cheesecake

This really is a delightful cheesecake – super rich and creamy with a crunchy biscuit base...

There's no cooking either, just chilling. Also, you can play around with this cake – add strawberries, or blueberries, change the type of biscuit for the base, add cinnamon, whatever you fancy.

Any way, it tastes like heaven on a plate. x

Serves 6
12 digestive biscuits
4oz butter
½ zest of a lemon
200ml Double cream
2 normal-sized tubs Philadelphia cream cheese (300 ml)
About 2 tablespoons caster sugar
1 tablespoon ground almonds
8-inch spring-sided cake tin

First melt the butter in a small bowl. I just put mine in the microwave for about 40 seconds or so – does the trick.

Next, break the biscuits. Either you can put them in a tea towel and smash them against something for a bit, or put them in a bowl and use the end of a rolling pin to bash them, but you want to really crumble them up nicely. When they are crumbled, pour in the melted butter and mix till the butter soaks into the biscuit. Then with the help of a spatula, put the mixture into the cake tin. Now spread that around till the surface is covered, and then use your fingers to press it down gently, making the surface as even as you can. Set aside.

Next, in a large bowl beat the cream till it starts to hold its shape, then add the tubs of cream cheese, almonds, lemon rind and sugar. Beat that together with a WOODEN SPOON (not a whisk) until it's all beautifully mixed in to a smooth creamy mixture. Now taste. Add more sugar if you feel it needs.

Again with the help of your trusty spatula, spoon and spread the cream cheese mixture over the biscuit base, trying to make it as even as possible. Place in the fridge for 3 hours and...

...Heaven awaits. x

MAN SIZE LASAGNE

If you're buying a T-shirt for a big man, you'd buy extra large, right? Well work on the same concept for this lasagne. I make this in extra large.

LARGE AMOUNTS. LARGE APPETITES.
TALK ABOUT FEED A MAN!

To make this, you'll need the recipe for bolognaise. Make the full amount as shown.

The white sauce is as follows:
200gms butter
2-2$\frac{1}{2}$ pints whole milk
5 heaped tablespoons flour
400gms grated gruyere cheese
Chunk of parmesan to grate over the top
...and of course you'll need the sheets of lasagne, 2 packs

First, make the bolognaise. I find the best thing to do is either make it early, or even the day before. Less hassle. But there are no rules, so long as you've given the bolognaise a nice long cooking time. Set to one side to cool.

When you're ready to make the white sauce, make sure you have everything to hand, cheese grated, milk out of the fridge, and so on. Also, you'll need a large non-stick saucepan, and a good whisk (by good, I mean metal, and not some useless plastic job)

OK, first melt the butter over a medium heat, and when it's almost melted, add the flour, a spoonful at a time, and stirring all the while. Once all the flour has been added, stir for about a minute or so. The mixture will look like a bubbling mass of sand. The posh name for this is a 'roux'. (If anyone asks how you made your white sauce, you can do a bit of showing off and say, 'well you just start with your basic roux...'!)

Anyway, once you've cooked this sandy-looking mixture for about 30 seconds or so, add a little of the milk. Use the whisk at this point, and don't worry if it looks lumpy and awful, it's supposed to. Just add a little more milk, and whisk it in. Keep whisking and add the rest of the milk a little at a time (any lumps should have all disappeared, but if they haven't, don't worry they will once the sauce starts to boil). So keep stirring, and you'll notice the sauce start to thicken as it gets hotter. Remember, you want a rich creamy sauce at pouring consistency, and the cheese will thicken it further, so if you feel at this point it's starting to look a little thick, add a little more milk.

Once the sauce has come to the boil, take it off the heat, and add the cheese. DON'T PUT IT BACK ON THE HEAT - just stir the cheese through. Once the cheese has melted, taste it, and season. Lovely, thick creamy cheesy sauce... mmmm

Now to assemble the lasagne is not hard. My 10-year-old son normally does it!

Get a large, deep-sided oven proof dish, and I mean large. I usually use a deep-sided oven tray!

If you've made the bolognaise the day before or earlier, you may need to add a drop of boiling water just to loosen it up. If not, just give it a good stir.

First spoon in some of the bolognaise, enough to cover the bottom of the tray. Then take the pasta sheets and place them side by side covering the meat sauce - you may need to play around snapping off bits of pasta sheets to fit. Oh, the fun you'll have! Don't know why I give all the best jobs to Jordan.

Next spoon over the cheese sauce, enough to cover, and repeat the process (but this time you get to do the snap and jigsaw bit with the pasta).

Then repeat the same thing (not going to get involved with your domestics as to who gets to do the last pasta layer) but this time on the top of the cheese sauce, grate over some parmesan.

You can cook this straight away, or about an hour before you're ready to serve, as with most things it's better to let it sit and just cool slightly before eating... makes for a much more enjoyable experience. Either way you'll need to put it into a pre-heated oven at 180°C/350°F/Gas Mark 4 for about 35 minutes or so, unless the instructions on the packet of pasta tell you different.

There you have it. An extra large dinner for all those extra large extra hungry men out there!

Tomato & Red Onion Salad

Lovely little salad this, great with BBQs, steak or chicken...

Not so great on the kissing front if you've got a hot date the next day. So, lovely as this salad is, eat it with your man... then kiss away!

1 red Onion
Roughly 5 or 6 beautiful largish Tomatoes
Olive Oil
White Wine Vinegar
Little squeeze of Lemon
Dijon Mustard
Salt
Pepper
Fresh Basil or Flat Leaf Parsley

Slice your tomatoes on their side, so you're left with lovely slices and no nasty top bit, and spread them over a lovely big serving plate.

Next slice your onion nice and thin (tears may happen, but there's nothing like a good cry), and scatter them over the tomatoes.

To make the dressing, take a little bowl and a fork, or if you have one, a sauce whisk, and into your bowl drop in a small dollop of Dijon Mustard. Add lots of salt and pepper and a couple of tablespoons of the White Wine Vinegar, and a 'little' squeeze of lemon. Give that a good mix, then add the Olive Oil. They say one part vinegar, three parts oil, but it's always best to go on taste, so add a little and Taste, Taste, Taste!

Pour the dressing over the tomatoes and onions, throw over the basil or parsley, and there you have it.

Big Kiss x

Whole Sea Bass with Roasted Cherry Tomatoes and New Potato Chips

This, in my opinion, is how fish should be eaten: Simple, Beautiful and purely Mediterranean.

Serves 4

1 large 2lb Sea Bass
1 large or 2 small packs of cherry tomatoes on the vine
Olive oil
Bunch of Fresh basil
1 large packet of new potatoes
Maldon rock salt
Ground black pepper
3 oven trays

Because we are using a whole fish, you will need to go to a fishmonger to get one. This is a good thing for many reasons. For a start, you get the size you need, it's fresh and lovely, and has not been anywhere near a nasty plastic container. Your charming monger will gut and de-scale it for you, but tell him to leave on the head and tail, as it looks so fantastically impressive when served. Of course, if your man is of the fishing breed, then just pack his sandwiches and send him out for the day to catch you one, but these gentlemen are few and far between, so fishmonger it is... you could always serve it wearing those rather sexy thigh-length wading boots though...

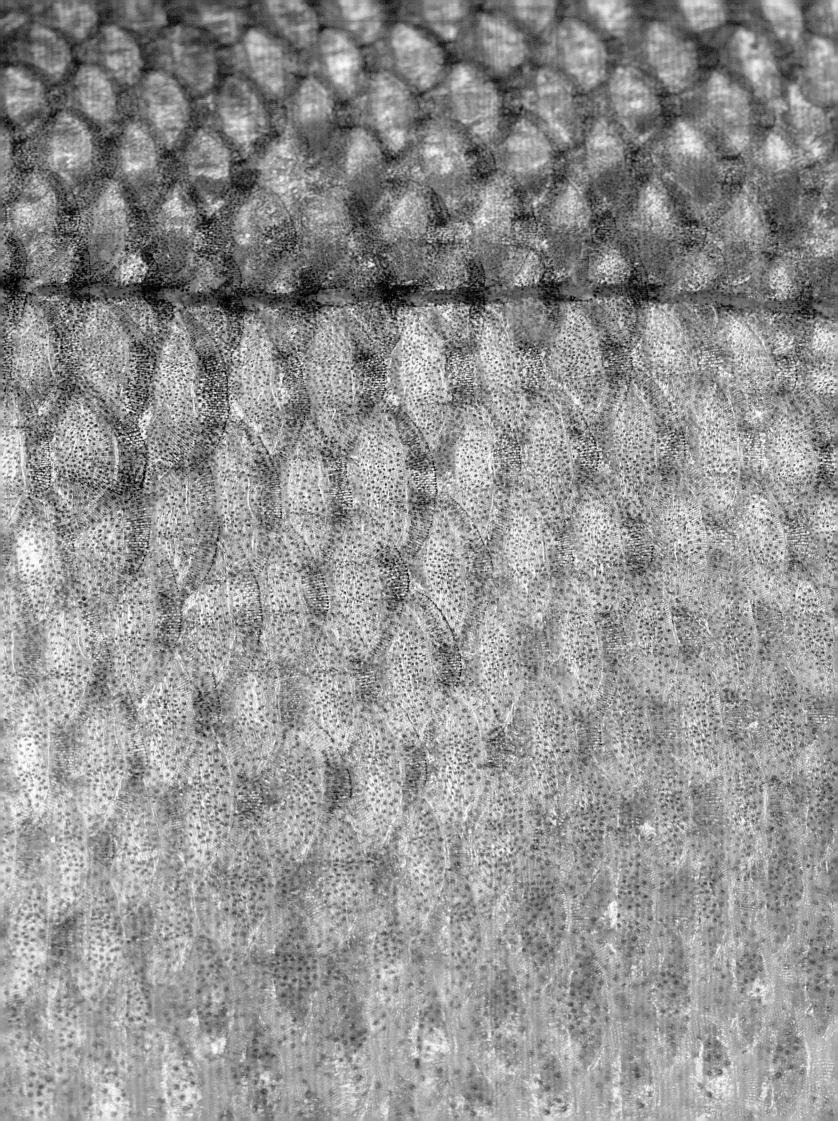

Right, now the first thing you should know is it takes literally minutes to cook a fish; in fact, this whole sea bass takes about 25 to 35 minutes, so DON'T put it in the oven till you are just about ready to serve.

In other words, you've had a nice large drink and a chat with whomever you've got coming, and all is relaxed and happy...

What you will need to do, though, (before that chat and drink) is get everything ready, and you'll be roasting the potatoes first, because they take double the cooking time, so start with them and pre-heat your oven to 200ºC/400ºF/Gas Mark 6.

Slice the new potatoes top to bottom – you want slightly longer slices – in quite thin slices. About 4 to 5 slices per potato, but don't go stressing if you come to a really small one and you can only get 3... This is, and should be, the very least of you worldly troubles.

Once done, throw the slices into an oven tray and drizzle olive oil all over them. Add some black pepper, and just give them a good toss around so they are all nicely coated, then arrange them flat on the oven tray. No salt at this point, salt comes about halfway through cooking time, and again at the end, but don't worry, I'll remind you. Put them in the oven, and they will take about 40 to 45 minutes. (If you do slice these guys up about an hour or so before you're ready to cook, just cover the oven tray with a tea towel. Don't worry too much if they discolour a little, you will never ever notice once they are cooked.)

Next, take your cherry tomatoes, and put them in the next oven tray. Absolutely leave them on their stalks. They look so beautifully natural like this, so don't change it. Again, drizzle over olive oil, and this time add plenty of salt and pepper. Roughly chop about a handful of basil, and throw it over the tomatoes, and give the tray a gentle shake to coat the tomatoes nicely.

Now with your beautiful fish, you really don't have to do very much… Simply place it in a large oven tray and rub all over with olive oil, salt and pepper. Sea bass has such a lovely delicate flavour that it really doesn't need any more than that. Just think Desert Island…

Once your potatoes have been in for roughly 20 minutes or so (they should be starting to get a lovely golden colour), take them out and sprinkle them with salt and give them a toss around, then put them back in the oven. At this point the fish and tomatoes go in too. Fish should be cooked in about 25 minutes, the last 10 of those minutes are going to be spent with the fish, and tomatoes, under a hot grill...

When there is 10 minutes left of cooking time, your potatoes should be just about done, so transfer them to the lowest shelf, and turn on the grill. Place the fish and tomatoes under the grill, if you can't fit both trays it's well worth your while to quickly transfer the tomatoes to the fish oven tray, saving the precious juices for later... What you're aiming for here is to crisp up the skin of the fish and scare the hell out of the tomatoes!

After 10 minutes under the grill the fish should have these lovely bubbles on the surface of the skin. If not, then give it a few more minutes – but only a few, you don't want to over cook it; big crime to do that. When it's ready take everything out of the oven and transfer the fish, with the help of a couple of fish slices to help you lift it, the tomatoes, still looking beautiful on their vine, and potato chips to the biggest serving plate you have, and pour over any juices from your tomato tray. Decorate the plate with a couple of small bunches of basil, and a few halved lemons, and walk like a Sicilian Mama to the table!

PS: Always put your best olive oil on the table, as well as salt and pepper, and drizzle a little over each serving of fish.

Simple. Healthy. Beautiful.

Box of Chocolates

Eating is a good thing.
Eating when you're sad, that's a good thing too, and don't
confuse sad as an excuse for greed. I mean sad as in the box of
chocolates, entire of course, but not the contents of the factory;

Eating is a good thing, and something so natural and good, that when you stop, really can't taste, can't swallow, and all that flows are tears, then you know it's bad. In those (hopefully not too often) times, reach for that box of chocolates. You may not eat them yet, but it's good to know they are there.

xx

STEAK
WITH
TERIYAKI
SAUCE

This sauce can be used with any steak. Being a South African girl myself, my personal favourite is a T-bone because you can have the best of both, the sirloin and the fillet. But rib-eye is just as good. I don't tend to buy rump though, because I always find it a bit tough.

The one thing I always do is buy my meat from a butcher and not pre-packaged from a supermarket, though I must say some supermarkets, particularly ones with their own butchers, are great...

But there is a difference, and besides, a butcher will always cut to your requirements. And if you're feeding a man, well none of those pre-packed centimetre thick jobs will do.

To my knowledge you'll need at least an inch to satisfy!

The Sauce

Good teaspoon of Wasabi
(green Japanese mustard)
Heaped teaspoon of wholegrain Dijon
mustard
Juice of 1½ lemons
¼-½ of a bottle Kikkoman Teriyaki marinade
(available in most supermarkets)
3 spring onions, finely sliced (green bit too)

Wasabi, being a mustard, is what gives this sauce
its kick. I'm not kidding when I say kick; a tablespoon
would probably blow your head off, and a little lick
would still give you a nudge you'd remember, so I think
a good teaspoon is all you'll need... unless of course
he's late home from the pub again and that old line
'your dinner's in the dog' is wearing thin. He won't
forget a tablespoon of this...

Anyway, to make the sauce, take a small bowl and
mix the Dijon mustard and the wasabi together, then
add the lemon juice. Pour in the teriyaki sauce and mix
again. Throw in the spring onions and taste. I love this
sauce quite lemony, but you do it to your taste. If it's
too hot, you can always add more teriyaki.

My mother makes loads of this sauce and keeps it in
a large jar in the fridge. It does only get better, which
I can vouch for as I do the same. When it runs low,
I simply top it up with fresh sauce, but never, ever
throw away....

HUNGRY YET

The Steak

Pre-heat your griddle pan, as always I say if you don't have one, get one... Rub salt and pepper onto your steak, and when your pan is seriously smoking hot, put your steak on.

Now watch it. Please, do not cremate this beautiful piece of meat, that really would be an utter shame, so watch the steak, and when the juices start to rise (you'll see what I mean when you're cooking it), turn it over, add a nice knob of butter to the top, and give it a little time on the other side, but not as much as the first side, depending on how thick it is. If you're at all worried, use the knife in your hand to cut into a little piece and have a look see, but bear in mind all meat needs time to sit and relax, if only for a minute or so, before eating, and during that time it will still be cooking...

BIG T-BONES ON A BIG PLATE...
BAKED POTATO WITH MELTED
BUTTER...TERIYAKI SAUCE
SPOONED OVER...

BOYS...? X

Laughing Potatoes

As all the best things in life seem to happen upon us unexpectedly, this way of baking potatoes did exactly that... The outcome was simply delicious. Read on...

I was at first simply baking my potatoes, as you would, in an oven tray, moderate oven, little drizzle of olive oil, for around 1 hour to 2 hours, depending on size. When I opened the oven to see how they were doing – you know, give them a little squeeze with the old oven glove – I happened to laugh at the same time as squeezing, and squeezed one a little too hard... The result was a rather messy version of a baked potato split down the middle without using a knife. I looked at him sitting there and looking for all the world like he desperately needed a bit of butter, almost asking me for a bit of butter, so I gave him some, a nice big knob, and then I did the same laughing squeezing thing to another couple of guys sitting next to him, and added butter to those too. I then returned the whole tray to the oven, turned the heat right up, and gave them all another 15 minutes or so.

The unsqueezed baked potatoes were, as you would imagine, like a normal baked potato, but the other guys, the ones with the squeeze, with the butter, let me tell you they were different class! Damn, they were good!

Needless to say, I have been baking potatoes this way ever since!

NB: You don't need to limit yourself by using your normal round baking potato, try using those long squiggly one that look like they've just come out of the ground.

Also, I know I've been very rough with the oven and time instructions, but that's because when the potatoes are in their skins like this, in a moderate oven, an exact time really doesn't have much relevance; so long as they have had a good hour, and are squeezable, it doesn't really matter when you decide to split them and add the butter. Even when you've turned the oven up, another 20 or even 25 minutes won't matter, it'll just crisp them up further...

A word of caution, though, I must add is this: Potatoes get hot. Really hot. I'm not kidding when I say I squeezed them with an oven glove. I did, and do, and I strongly suggest that you do too!

Fillet on Mustard
with
Rocket

When I was a little girl, I would watch my Father standing in the kitchen making this. He would have made it with a leftover Sunday roast, or fillet of beef, or even last night's steak…

I remember feeling hungry just seeing this great big man with his great big hands, slicing steak, and spreading mustard. He'd say to me, "Stash, this is how they do it in Italy!"

Whether this is strictly true or not never bothered me, but it surely developed my love of simplicity. Great food, made simply and tasting fantastic. Thanks, Dad. x

Nowadays, I love this dish so much, and eat it so often, that I don't wait for leftovers, but buy fillet steaks and griddle them in advance of when I need them… The rest is simply assembly!

Here's how:
3 or 4 fillet steaks (can use sirloin as well, or even rib eye)
3-4 forkfuls of English Mustard
1 juicy Lemon
1 packet Rocket
Olive Oil
Salt
Pepper

First, if you're not working with leftovers, you need to griddle your
steaks. Make sure the griddle pan is 'smoking hot'. Salt and
pepper the steaks, and place on the hot pan. These guys
should take about 2 minutes on either side (less for a thinner steak).
The thing you need to know when making steak is that it is
an absolute crime to overcook them. Really it is. I've converted many a
person who said they wanted their steak well done, by simply ignoring
them, and giving it to them medium to rare.
Never had a complaint, and I'm pleased to say
they've had it that way ever since.

When making a steak, you really only need to turn it once. When you
first put it on the griddle, just leave him there and don't bother him.
Once you see the blood start to appear, turn him over, add a knob of
butter to the cooked side, and give him another
minute or two to cook.

If you are at all unsure, or if you think you'll be committing the
'over-cooking' crime, just cut into it to see how it's doing. With this
particular recipe you need to cook it even less than you would normally,
because the steak is not going to be eaten straight away. Instead, it will
be sitting happily, UNCOVERED, on a plate till you're ready. (I stress
uncovered, because if you take this beautifully cooked piece of meat,
then cover him in foil, he will continue to
cook at a greater rate than if you just leave him, and you
will be most disappointed when you go to slice it
and it's completely over-done. Not good.)

It really does not matter if there are hours between you making the
steaks and eating them. In fact, they have to be room temperature.
I usually have this on a night where I've made steak for the
kids for dinner, cooked them all at the same time,
and just left mine and my lover's for later…

Now the steak-making rules have been explained, and you have your children in bed and your perfectly cooked fillets awaiting you, the fun part starts…

Take a large serving plate, and using a fork, scoop out some mustard, and spread onto the plate as evenly as you can. I know English mustard is hot, but believe me, this is not a hot dish, just a damn tasty one. Make sure the plate is covered, if you need more mustard, because your plate is particularly large, use it. Once done, salt and pepper, and a lovely healthy drizzle of olive oil on top of the mustard.

Next we slice the steaks. Use a sharp knife and cut the slices about half a centimetre thick. You'll find that because the steak has been sitting pretty for a while, slicing is easy peasy.
Lay the slices first around the widest part of the plate, and then the next layer under that and so on, so you have kind of fanned out the steak.

Now take the rocket, and simply scatter and pile the leaves on top of the steak. Then, again, salt and pepper, squeeze over your juicy lemon, and drizzle with olive oil.
Fresh and lovely, and wonderful served with a tomato and avocado salad.

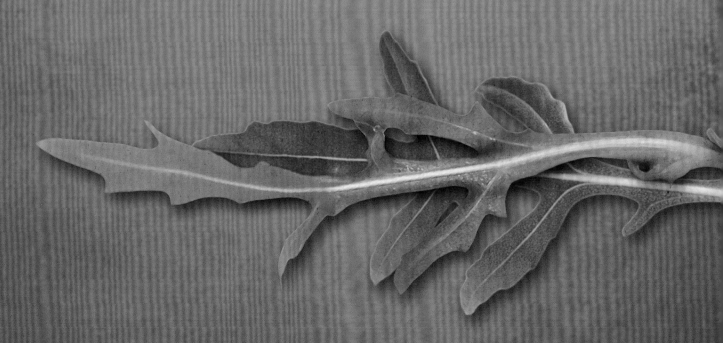

Ma's Avocado and Tomato Salad

*One of my Mother's creations... honestly never
seen it fail to please. Serve with meat,
chicken or fish.*

Just wonderful.

*Handful of vine tomatoes (though you can use any
tomatoes really, so long as they are sweet and fresh)
Couple of ripe avocados
Dijon mustard
Good Balsamic Vinegar
Olive oil
Salt
Pepper*

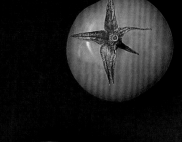

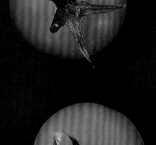

*Halve or quarter the tomatoes
depending on their size, and put
in a largish bowl. Next, halve
the avos, take the stone out,
(bang the knife into the stone
and gently twist), then holding
the avocado in your hand take a
spoon and scoop it out into the
bowl with the tomatoes...
Easy peasy.*

*Now the dressing is also really
easy, and you make it in the
bowl with the avos and
tomatoes. Simply take a large
salad server and place it in
the bowl so that the spoon
is facing you (because in
this spoon is where you'll be
making your dressing), and
into the spoon put lots of salt
and pepper, a nice dollop of
mustard, and then pour in the
Balsamic. It's hard to be exact
about measurements here, so I
really strongly suggest you taste
the vinegar BEFORE you add it*

*so you have an idea as to how
sweet or sharp it is. A good
Balsamic is sweet, and this salad
can take quite a bit. So, pour
the vinegar into the spoon, not
worrying if some escapes into
the salad, and then using a fork,
give the mustard and vinegar a
little mix in the large salad spoon.*

*Next pour some lovely olive
oil into the spoon, tip it into
the salad once, twice, and once
more, then give the whole thing
a good mix. Now TASTE! It
may well be that you need a
little more salt or Balsamic in
which case add it...*

*Don't worry if the avos mush
slightly round the edges, this
is what you want. Also, unlike
most salads, this can be made a
little in advance. Nothing wilts,
it just gets tastier, just give it
another toss before you serve
it. x*

For Ladies Who Lunch...

Chicken Breasts with Rocket and Parmesan

If you're feeding a hungry man, you can always serve some little new potatoes, but as healthy as this is, I promise you it is very filling! Great for a 'Ladies' Lunch' too.

Please feel free to play with your marinade too. For example, I sometimes add nice hot green chillies, or some fresh thyme... The chicken too does not always need to be served on top of rocket leaves; a warm bed of rice is also a lovely place for your chicken to sit. xx

Chicken breasts with Rocket and Parmesan

This is my answer to clean healthy living. Not sure, but it can't have many calories in it for those of you that count. I don't. Being totally dyslexic with numbers is my excuse!

Serves 2
3 chicken breasts
Bag of rocket salad
Olive oil
Couple of lemons
Balsamic vinegar (optional)
Parmesan shavings
Salt
Pepper

Take a large serving plate and spread with the rocket leaves. Season with salt and pepper.
Griddle pan. If you don't have one, get one they are fantastic, or else use a non-stick frying pan.
Take your chicken breast, lay it flat and place your hand on the top. Carefully slice into the middle of it with a sharp knife, but don't cut all the way through it. Open it up and you should have a sort of heart shape. Ah, sweet. Now take a rolling pin and give it a bit of a bash to flatten slightly. Once done, put the breasts into a dish, season with salt (only if you're ready to cook now, if not then just before you throw them on the grill add salt) and pepper, squeeze over some lemon juice, and lug in some olive oil. Get your hands in and rub the chicken all over.
It can sit like this for as long as you like, or can be cooked straight away...

Your pan should be good and hot, literally smoking hot before you place the chicken on it. While the chicken is cooking – it doesn't take very long, about 5 to 8 minutes or so – squeeze lemon and drizzle oil over the rocket leaves. Check the chicken, remember you want to end up with lovely juicy chicken and not something shrivelled, dried and nasty that not even the cat would eat, so once you've turned it, cut into the fattest part. It should be white, but still juicy.

When your chicken is ready, put it on top of the rocket leaves. Throw over a handful of parmesan shavings, bit more olive oil and a squeeze of lemon, little splash of balsamic vinegar, and serve!

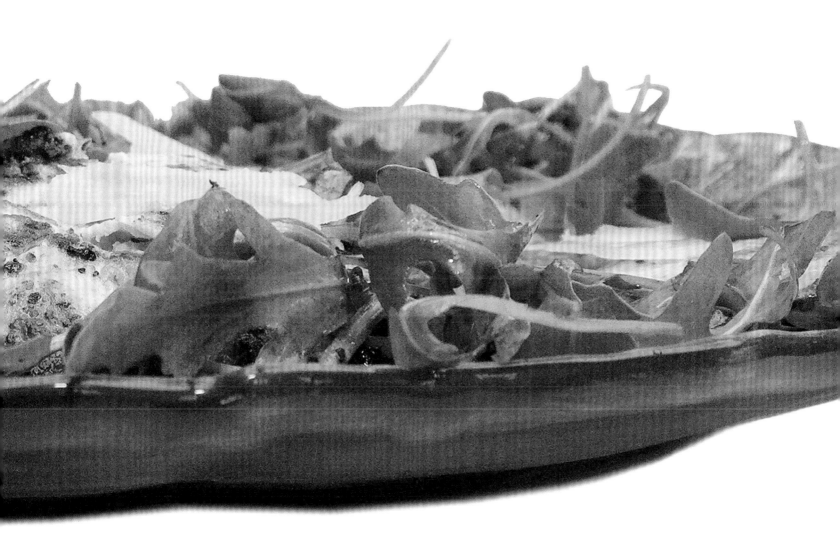

Beautiful
Banana Bread...

I say banana bread, but really it's a cake. I guess the reason for my confusion is that it's baked in a loaf tin, and is truly wonderful sliced, smothered in butter, and eaten in the morning with a nice cup o' tea; though perfectly lovely with that afternoon cup too!

Also, if you're anything like me, and try to do the healthy thing occasionally by buying loads of beautiful yellow bananas, only to watch them turn into nasty brown has-beens, then this is the perfect way to use them!

4oz butter
6oz brown sugar
8oz flour, sieved
2 eggs
1 teaspoon baking powder
2 tablespoons milk
2 large soft bananas, sliced
Nutmeg
Cinnamon

Pre-heat the oven to 150°C/300°F/Gas Mark 2

Take your loaf tin, and with a bit of kitchen paper, rub softened butter all over the inside. Then, pour in some caster sugar, and shake the tin around so the sugar sticks to the butter, and your tin is nicely coated. Before you begin, weigh out all the ingredients, and add the baking powder to the flour. Much easier and quicker this way, and less chance of leaving something out. I watched *Blue Peter*, so I know.

OK, in a large mixing bowl, combine the butter and the sugar. I use electric beaters for this cake, but you can use a good old-fashioned wooden spoon if you like. Add the bananas, and mix with the butter and sugar. If at this point, or at any point for that matter, the mixture starts to split, or separate, don't panic, help is at hand in the name of flour. Just throw some in, and keep mixing, if it still looks nasty, add a bit more. Don't worry, it will come right.

Now when you add the eggs, do it slowly. Not sure what the rules are here, but I always add a little egg, then a little flour, and so on, until it's all combined. Then add the milk and mix that in too.

Now with the cinnamon and nutmeg, you can add as much or as little as you like. I'm a bit of a cinnamon freak, so I add lots, but this is your banana bread, so you decide. The best way to do this is to taste it, before and after you have added the spices... and what a naughty little privilege that is!

Right, in the oven for an hour, hour-ten, then leave to cool in the tin. Well, you're supposed to, but I challenge any of you to leave this lovely bread sitting there waiting to go stone cold, when you could be eating it warm, with the butter melting into it... Cup o' tea anyone?

...and a nice

cup o' tea

STICKY BBQ RIBS

A FATHER DAUGHTER COMBO

How to feed a man? This is it. It almost seems to transport them back to a Neanderthal era. I have actually seen one or two lose the power of speech, and communicate in some kind of grunting noise! But far from being disturbing, it's really quite wonderful to watch. I also think the fact that they have barbecued them themselves over hot coals only adds to the hype. (Warning: if your man decides to wear his loin cloth whilst barbecuing, please do make sure his vital parts are safely protected!)

Serves 4-6 (or 3 starving cavemen)
20 pork ribs
½ large onion
Roughly 20 peppercorns (you really don't have to actually count them out, that would be a sad act indeed)
5 bay leaves

BBQ Sauce
500ml ketchup (1 bottle)
Juice of 1 orange
3 teaspoons English Mustard
125ml HP Sauce
4 large tablespoons Golden Syrup
3 tablespoons BBQ HP Sauce
1 teaspoon Tabasco Sauce
2 large tablespoons soft brown sugar

Now I've called this a 'Father/Daughter combo' 'cos my Dad taught me that if you don't boil the ribs first, no matter how great the sauce is it just won't be any good. And he's absolutely right, because from boiling them first comes wonderfully tender meat that just falls off the bone… seriously good.

Another fantastic thing about these ribs is you can make them well in advance of actually barbecuing them, and because they have been boiled and are already cooked, the act of barbecuing at the end is simply to add that special BBQ flavour, and slightly blacken and caramelize the edges.

So first we start by boiling the ribs. Take the largest pot you have, fill with hot water, and put on to boil. You can rinse the ribs in cold water first if you like, but this isn't entirely necessary.

Put the ribs, onion, peppercorns and bay leaves into the pot, and bring to the boil. You'll notice a lot of not particularly nice stuff start to rise and sit on the surface of the water, but don't worry. Just take a large spoon, and 'skim' around the surface, discarding any yuckiness in a little bowl (it's a good idea to keep this spoon and bowl to hand, as you'll probably have to skim a few more times). Turn the heat down to a simmer, cover with a lid, but leave a little gap, and that's all you need do for the next hour and a half, except maybe a bit of skimming, which is no real hardship.

Now while that's cooking, you can get on and make your BBQ sauce. Totally easy, just pour, add and mix all listed ingredients into a very large bowl (I say large because when your ribs are cooked, you can just throw them into same bowl as the sauce). If you don't make the sauce, then mix in the big saucepan you cooked your ribs in.

Once the ribs are cooked (test one by taking it out and cutting into a little chunk – it should fall away quite easily), drain them into a colander, throw out the onion, bay leaves and as many peppercorns as you can find, and then, like I said, just tip the whole lot into that fabulous sauce!

Mix it all around, I find hands are by far the best method of mixing, and set aside till your salivating Caveman speaks the words: "Shall I light the fire?"

After the fire is lit and the coals nice and hot, it really should be left to him to deal with, but in case his loincloth does start to smoulder, here's what you do:

Simply place the ribs on the BBQ using tongs. They won't take too long to do because they are already cooked, but you do want to get them lovely and caramelized, so just keep turning them this way and that till you are satisfied. He will love you FOREVER. x

Homemade Potato Salad

I've called this 'homemade' potato salad because there really is such a big difference between this and any kind of shop-bought or deli-bought stuff. I don't quite know exactly why this is, I just know it's so. Obviously it's great as a picnic food, but goes seriously well with my BBQ ribs... You could also have it as a fridge raid and eat it just by itself!!

Serves around 6-8
2 little tubs, or 1kg little new potatoes (can use gorgeous Jersey Royals too)
Roughly 300ml (just a little less than half a 650ml jar) of mayonnaise
4 spring onions, finely chopped
1 tablespoon olive oil
Little squeeze of lemon
Salt and pepper

Boil the potatoes in a big pot of salted water for around 15 to 20 minutes. I normally take one out after 15, cut it in half and have a little bite. You'll know when they are cooked because the inside will still have texture, but no crunch.

While the potatoes are boiling away, get a large bowl and put in the mayo, olive oil, chopped spring onions, and salt and pepper. Squeeze in just a little lemon juice, but not too much. You don't want to taste the lemon, but just have it there to give it a little secret something... You can always add more at the end should you need it. OK, now don't mix that yet, just leave it sitting pretty in your bowl looking like something off a Delia Smith programme. Trés professional...

Once your potatoes are cooked, drain them in a colander, and just run cold water over them for a minute or so; this stops them cooking, but leaves them nice and warm, and easy to handle, which is exactly what we want. So, now put the colander next to your bowl (the one that you prepared earlier... we go all *Blue Peter* now) with the mayo etc in it. Roughly cut the larger potatoes in half, and toss them into the bowl. What I do as well is actually squish a couple of them in my hands. Not only does this seem to add to the whole 'homemade' feeling, but it's an extremely childish act, and therefore very satisfying!

When all the potatoes are in, take a large spoon and gently give the whole thing a good mix. And this is where I think the magic comes in... because the potatoes are still warm, the mayo seems to embrace the potatoes as a lover would in a way that it just doesn't do when they are cold... Everything goes all beautifully creamy and lovely... Please taste it now, just in case it does need that extra tiny squeeze of lemon, or perhaps salt, but other than that, you're done. Keep it out the fridge in a cool place till you're ready to serve it. Yummy. xx

Mummy   What do you love about me?

Well let's see 'said Mummy,

I love your eyes because they twinkle when you laugh.

I love your mouth because it kisses me

I love your bellybutton because it belongs only to you

I love your fingers because they wave 'Hello'

I love your toes because they wiggle when I tickle them

And

I love your ears, because they hear me say -

'I love you'

I love your toes

FIGHT FOR PEACE WITH

LOVE

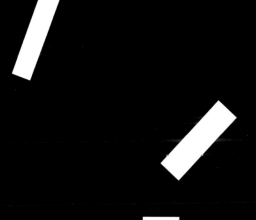
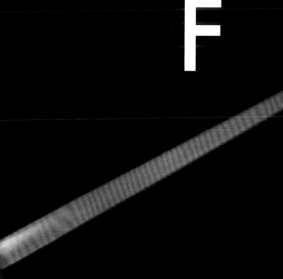

I would like to say Thank You to the following people. People without whom I wouldn't be the Person I am, and People who made it all happen.

Tony Freeth – you really are as your company says, Damnfine. Forever I will remember the hours we spent doing the ridiculous and the impossible. No challenge was ever too large for you, no idea too crazy. When I say I couldn't have done it without you, I add I wouldn't have wanted to either. x

My Darling Babies...
Just stay and Grow as Beautiful as you Are.
In Good times and bad my Darlings,
Everyday, and Each Night,
You are Always My Reason.
I love you xxx

Daddy, you showed me from the start
what a Wonderful thing Food is.
Food and Life, and How to Live it...
See the Beauty, Feel the Love...
Share the Laughter
You are all of This and More.
You have given me This, and More;
I know I shall run out of pages before
I begin to tell just how much that is.
I Love you Daddy, so much x

Mama, to simply say Thank You would never ever cover it. There is no beginning and no end.
It's everyday. Everyday x
I Love you Mama x

Thank you to my Darling StepFather, who is always there when I really need him... and need him I do xxx

To Each and Everyone of my Friends... Never, not once, has any one of you let me down. Without you few I would have nothing to share. With you Few, I have the World, and all its gathered Wisdom.
I love you all, very much x

Thank You Karl for Seeing and Believing;
There is such Strength in that.
You truly are the Gladiator

Zenon, You are True to the Power,
Heart and Imagination your Name holds.
The Good that's in you comes through in
your Photographs.
Thank you for allowing me to Push to the Limit...
And taken with such Grace x

Lindsey, Darling you are just so very pretty xxx

Thank You Howard x

Thank You Legs x

And finally, to Everyone who Kindly allowed me to use their Image...
You have made this book what it is –
Thank You and God Bless you All
x

First published in 2010 by Opus Media Group

All rights reserved. No part of this publication may be reproduced or transmitted in any form or by any means, or stored in any retrieval system of any nature without prior written permission of the copyright holders, except for permitted fair dealing under the Copyright, Designs and Patents Act 1988.

The information in this book is based on material supplied to Opus Media Group. While every effort has been made to ensure accuracy, Opus Media Group does not under any circumstances accept responsibility for any errors or omissions.

Opus Media Group have made all reasonable efforts to reach artists/photographers and/or copyright owners of images used in this book. We are prepared to pay fair and reasonable fees for any usage made without compensation or agreement.

Opus Media Group shall not be liable for any loss or claim in connection with any injury or other damage resulting from the use or handling of this book, save that this shall in no way exclude or limit the liability of Opus Media Group for death or personal injury resulting from its own negligence.

A Cataloguing-in-Publication record for this book is available from the Publisher.

ISBN 978-1-905794-29-4

Printed and bound in China

Image Credits

Zenon Texeira, KrakenCreative – Front Cover Stasha; Stasha's Thank You to L (Hair and make-up: Annette Field www.annettefield.com); Sunflower Plate; Sea Salt; Grey Poupon Mustard Lid; Teriyaki Sauce Bottle; Frying Pan; Manuel Candle; Blue Sky with Clouds; 1950s Housewife in Kitchen (Model: Lyndsey); Sensitive Mushroom; Lucozade Bottle; Provence Sunflower Landscape; Peoni Flowers; Clock; Cloudy Sky; Stasha as Cake Bunny; Bow Tie; Legs; Spaghetti; Lazy Sunday Armchair; Pie; Mini (Digital Retouching: Martin Sully); Man Bath Still Life; Stasha on Magazine Cover (Hair and make-up: Annette Field); Hair Brush and Perfume Bottles; Butter in Pan; Tabouli; Runny Marmalade; Mafioso Eating at Table (Model: Howard Forrester); Empty Plate; Jelly Beans; Frilly Pink Knickers; Running Shoe (Supplied by: Coventry Runner); Seascape; Chocolate Heart; Colman's Jar; Children's Shoes; Marmalade Jars; Teriyaki Chicken; Avocado and Tomato Salad; Mango and Passion Fruit; Mama Burger; Chicken Breast with Rocket and Parmesan; Lasagne; Carrot Cake; Provencal Tart; 20-Minute Lamb.

Martin Sully, Kraken Creative – Breakfast Café Sauce Bottles; Bread; Lifts; Whiskey Bottle and Tumbler.

Matt Crockford, Kraken Creative – Caveman; Marlon Brando; La Fede Tin; Fuel Empty and Fuel Full.

Design Concept by Stasha Butterfly & Tony Freeth
Creative Design and Initial Visualisation by Tony Freeth & Stasha Butterfly
Creative design development by Kraken Creative – Creative Director: Zenon Texeira
Senior Design Team: Matt Crockford and Martin Sully

J. Helgason Typewriter; **David Politzer-Ahles** Olive Oil; **Eline Spek** Buttercup; **FloridaStock** Chair; **Radovan Spurny** Taj Mahal; **fat_fa_tin** Wallpaper; **Graeme Dawes** Mushrooms; **Mr McHaddock** Ortiz Tin; **Elnur Drink** Daisies; **R** Field of Buttercups; **Sean Nel** Well; **Peter Dankov** Rose; **David W Hughes** Rubber Ducks; **Neale Cousland** Angel Statue; **Nanka (Kucherenko Olena)** Angel Feather; **Norman Chan** Green Salad; **Michael Steden** Vintage Book; **Tom Robbrecht** Green Apples; **Geoff Hardy** Pickle; **PhotoStocker** Orange Butterfly; **Netfalls** Boat; **Stelian Ion** Santorini; **Andreas G. Karelias** Old Greek Lady; **Paul Cowan** Roast potatoes; **Feng Yu** Mangos; **Flavijus** Spoon; **Chris Sargent** Ginger Tom; **Melanie DeFazio** Asparagus; **Cameilia** Chicken; **Balaikin** Picture Frames; **Jasmina007** Blossom; **Tony Freeth** Lamb Sprinters; Wedding Salmon, Apple Bath, Forest and Honey Bath, Poached Pears (Banana Bread and Tuna Pasta Fish Hook both from original creations by Tony Freeth); **Nikkytok** Violin; **Jennifer Bremer** Wishing Well Motel; **Klara Salamonska** www.flickr.com/photos/chmurka/ Chmurka (Hamster); **Jonathan Larsen** Rugby Player, Sportlibrary Rugby Player; **Paul Cowan** Red Onion; **Ton Vols** Sea Bass Scales; **Amanda Clements** Sunset; **José Aguirre** www.flickr.com/photos/13328582@N00/ Dog in Glasses; **Jennifer Stone** Potatoes; **Studio Araminta** Cherry Tomatoes in Heart; **Mikhail Pogosov** Edwardian Lady; **Patrizia Tilly** Ladybird; **Taratorki** Rocket Leaves; **Shipov Oleg** Fish Hook; **Morgan Lane Photography** Banana; **BW Folsom** Bread; **Margie Hurwich** China Cup; **David Hughes** Country Landscape; **Veronika Vasilyuk** Abstract; **Lily** Heart in Pastels.

I
will wait for
my Star,
But
when it comes,
I'm
Determined to
make it
Shine.

An Explanation of Sorts

People so often ask the question "why did you write this? What inspired you?" Simple enough and inevitable question, but funnily enough not all that easy to answer. I could I suppose genuinely answer both in a word "Love." But would that be enough of an explanation? Sadly not, and I put the word sadly because in my Utopia, my Fairy tale world that I love to live in, it's perfectly clear, and more than enough explanation, it wouldn't have even been a question. Love. One small word, The maker of all that emotion. Laughter, tears, sorrow, joy; Depth that you never knew you had. Love. Strived for. Dreamt of. Lusted after. Love. Creator and genius. Binding, longing, and living for. I mean, seriously, what are we all here for if not to feel it. Mother, brother, sister, Father, child, friend, lover, husband. What's it all for if not this one small word.

So you see, it was all of these things and more that inspired, no compelled me to write this book. It was simply making something really yummy for dinner and receiving ooohs and arrhs, and wonderfully well-fed and happy looks that made me take to my really old computer and tap tap out the letters one by one, which turned into writing, which I remembered I really liked to do because there is such wonderful freedom in writing, and you find this voice, and it's so honest, it has to be because there is only you in the room, and what you're writing is very important because it is from the Heart, and the Heart is always honest, and besides, I was writing recipes with measured out stuff, and oven temperatures and all sorts, and there is no way I would want to put you wrong, I would feel really bad about that, because you see I'm really and truly not a chef, I just love to cook, and I still get nervous before a dinner party, and I really should probably push myself to do more things, and I'm sure at some point I will, maybe, but the things in this book I cook all the time. I make the food in here for my babies and my man and my friends. And I Love all of them.

Now once the words were written I had to colour them in, and I do so like colouring! More than that, I really don't like things to be the same old. My beloved Man had once given me the key to this door of creation, and once opened, I've since lost the key, and Narnia is looking great! I love it in here!

I decided I wanted to do more than go down the recipe one side photo the other side route, so I had to think straight out of the box… I love that extra mile! I cannot tell you how much fun I had! Loopy loopy ideas, madness out of no where - escaped! Working all the hours with the wonderful Tony Freeth as the colour in my finger tips, him constantly telling me I was nuts, and me constantly laughing. Gosh it was fun. Never even really even felt like work, though I often shouted just for the hell of the "can't you see I'm working!"

Then one day I had a book. Pages and everything. Opus found me, and I found someone who got what I was about and didn't try to change it, and for this I will always be grateful.

My book. Written because all I had in me was to write, filled right up to the top with love, and I just wanted to share. And share it now I do with you.
I hope, in the very least, it at some point makes you smile.
X

x

Ps. Called it *How to Feed a Man* because men are simply the best creatures to feed… though a pack of hungry kids comes a close second x